T0196472

Author photo credit

Tania Cafasso

Cover Graphics/Art Credit

Frank Stillitano from Flux

"Death anxiety is a major issue facing Western society, but with Joy Nugent's latest title, *Parting the Veil – Reflections on Soul*, it need not be so. As Joy eloquently puts it, 'Get death right, and you get life right.' Understanding death and dying is therefore as much about living in this moment as it is about the journey into the next stage of existence. Joy's book will not only help you find peace with death and dying, it will also help you find peace in this lifetime."

Dr. Scott Zarcinas
Author of *Your Natural State of Being*

"The author describes music and art as the language of the soul. Her first palliative care course for nurses in 1988 included presentations on art and music therapies, demonstrating her focus on the whole person and her belief that the unconscious and the soul, as well as physical and social concerns, must be considered in end of life care. It was a privilege to be involved in a conference exploring complementary therapies that she coordinated in Sandakan, East Malaysia. Eastern philosophy with a belief in reincarnation has been central to her own path."

Nancy Caldwell
Retired Art Therapist

Parting the Veil

REFLECTIONS ON SOUL

Joy Nugent

BALBOA.PRESS
A DIVISION OF HAY HOUSE

Balboa Press books may be ordered through booksellers or by contacting:

Balboa Press
A Division of Hay House
1663 Liberty Drive
Bloomington, IN 47403
www.balboapress.com
AU TFN: 1 800 844 925 (Toll Free inside Australia)
AU Local: 0283 107 086 (+61 2 8310 7086 from outside Australia)

Print information available on the last page.

ISBN: 978-1-5043-1361-2 (sc)
ISBN: 978-1-5043-2342-0 (hc)
ISBN: 978-1-5043-1362-9 (e)

Balboa Press rev. date: 11/11/2020

CONTENTS

Author of

As Good As Goodbyes Get: A Window into Death and Dying
and
My Way: One Nurse's Passion for End of Life

ACKNOWLEDGEMENT

I wish to acknowledge my many mentors and guides—seen and unseen.

In particular, I wish to thank Ian Maddocks AM, Emeritus Professor of Palliative Care, Flinders University, South Australia. Ian was generous in his willingness to participate in the educational programs NurseLink Foundation, promoted both in Australia and in East and West Malaysia, as well as seeing patients when needed.

Also, Michael Barbato, a Palliative Care Physician for over two decades in New South Wales. He was introduced to me through a newspaper article naming him a Death Whisperer. He was a guest presenter for several of my educational programs, and his writings in mystical experiences and deathbed visions inspired me.

In addition to four children who are positively making their own mark on the world, I have twelve grandchildren whose inquiring minds keep me searching for simple ways to explain the profound truths that I am learning.

My home-based private nursing career could not have been possible without the support of my caring team of nurses and palliative care assistants who offered a "professional family" style of care.

FOREWORD

Joy Nugent - a woman ahead of her time!

As the oldest of her four children, I have the honor of introducing our mother and her latest thoughts on the final stages of life and beyond.

Ever since she was a youngster, Joy has been one to seek and embrace new challenges and to welcome with a gapingly open mind different spiritual philosophies and ways of seeing things.

Brought up in a strict Methodist family, she agreed enthusiastically to attend a boarding school some hundreds of kilometres away. She took the opportunity as soon as she finished her nursing studies to travel to the far side of the world.

When motherhood arrived she threw herself into being the best mother she possibly could. Part of this involved revamping the traditional family diet of the 1970s to include other healthy and varied options; I remember she was the first of her friends to put aside suspicion and purchase a new type of oven which cooked via 'microwaves'!

She made sure she put her energies into creating the best birthday parties for her children. She made costumes and created party themes which flowed on to uproarious games - all in keeping with the fantasy envisaged. Fairy bread, chocolate crackles and mountains of other sugary treats were forgotten as we wolfed down our attractively presented healthy options, eager to get on with the next pirate, swagman or safari themed activity.

Part of her maternal style also involved less popular disciplines, such as limited television and a refusal to let her children be satisfied by mediocre performances. She threw us into learning musical instruments and attending ballet and art classes as soon as we could walk just on the off chance that one of us may have some prodigal talents in these areas! This was not the case, however we all benefitted greatly from the exposure to new and different places, people and pursuits.

With kids trickling out of the home in the 1980's, she re-discovered time in her day, retrained as a nurse and then found her calling in the fledgling field of Palliative Care. She quickly learned that the patient needed to be put back into the centre of the dying process, and the various aspects that make us human, such as our physical, spiritual, intellectual and psychological needs, all demanded fulfillment at this stage of our lives.

Over the years of her involvement with palliative care she would draw inspiration from past pioneers in her field, with Florence Nightingale and Elisabeth Kubler–Ross being her heroes of their day. Joy also, however, respected Eastern philosophies and the part they have played in healing body, mind and soul. Caroline Myss, Jeffrey Allen and Thomas Hubl are modern day mystics who inspire!

Like a ninja warrior, she developed a Zen–like knack of deflecting her conservative critics who scoffed at her gullibility and unfashionable enthusiasm for new age 'weirdness'. Since that time though, healing arts such as acupuncture, hypnosis, reiki and others have found their way more and more into the toolbox of the mainstream therapist.

It will thus not surprise, when in the future, health and well-being practitioners will look closely at now fringe philosophies such energy medicine and various meditation techniques and say to themselves, 'Isn't this the stuff that Joy Nugent was espousing all those years ago?'

INTRODUCTION

> Everyone has a purpose in life... a unique gift or special
> talent to give to others. And when we blend this unique
> talent with service to others, we experience the ecstasy
> and exultation of our own spirit, which is the ultimate
> goal of all goals.
>
> —Deepak Chopra

In this book, I share my soul's journey, and, like so many people in the
last phase of life, I may repeat events from previous writing, which, I feel,
still lack integration into my *truth*.

"Parting the veil" is a common metaphor for the transition from life to
death. When I visited the Scottish Island of Iona, I learned that Scottish
kings liked to be buried on the island, as it was considered that the veil
between worlds was the thinnest in that part of Scotland. Religious texts
and myths would have us believe that the souls of all mankind lived with
God (however one perceives the unknowable cosmic energy that gives
energy to life) before their birth. Going home, or returning to where we
came from is a common instinctual desire that is expressed in many ways.
It seems to be in our DNA. When in a stressful and frightening situation,
many of us turn to God in prayer or cry out for the archetypical mother. I
know in my own life, as a mother of four and grandmother of twelve, that
I receive more visits when my children and grandchildren are experiencing
uncertainty. When I receive no messages from family, I take it as a sign
that all is well with them. I strive to let go, and my daily prayer is for God
to hover over them and to protect them. I have often said to those in the
bedside vigil of a person who is dying that to love is to let go.

The Swiss psychiatrist Dr. Elisabeth Kubler-Ross taught the world so much about death and dying. She wrote that the "moment of transition" is a natural and painless process for the dying person, and is usually experienced a being something wonderful. I like to view it as a threshold into another stage of the life of my soul. Yet, the transition from life to death is feared and avoided at all costs by so many. While working in a hospice, I met a gentleman who shared with me the arrangements he had made for his funeral. At the time, I was wearing the blue uniform of a refresher student and was surprised to be called aside by one of the permanent staff and told not to encourage such a conversation as it might depress the patient. Denial of death takes many forms.

Letting go of the need to know and trusting in unseen influences needs practice and faith. The consciousness of a larger view is attained through education and awareness. We are in an age when life is revered and protected. Yet, if Life and Death are one, as the sages say, it is the natural place of Death to beg the same respect currently given to Life. Death is not the enemy! It is a part of life and needs to be understood rather than feared. The soul knows when it is time for the body to die. For many of us, fear of what comes next interferes with the celebration of death as a life event.

Legislation before many parliaments around the world denies people the right to die as they wish and imposes restrictions - rightly or wrongly - on physician-assisted dying. These restrictions rely on a psychiatrist and a disease prognosis to be the gatekeeper. It is true that what affects one affects the whole, and caution and deliberation is wise. Humans are more than bodies and minds - "we are spiritual beings having a physical experience."

These are the words of Pierre Teilhard de Chardin, a French philosopher and a Jesuit priest. He trained as a paleontologist and geologist, and took part in the discovery of Peking Man. His work, like so many others, combines science and spirituality. I like to take a cosmic view of life, as well as the view that we are souls travelling through many lifetimes. Mystical teacher Thomas Hubl gave me the idea that we do not have a soul but rather a soul has us. The "us" is a physical body, an emotional body and a mental body. The soul is eternal and is the part of us that does not die.

Author Barbara Marx Hubbard, who admired Pierre Teilhard de Chardin, writes about the awakening of a new species of man that moves from individual ego recognition of responsibility to a consciousness that is infused with all living creatures. This means that we do not kill or harm another person because that person is a part of us! Legislation on the concept of physician-assisted dying and the fear of the slippery slope would take on a new outlook if there was consideration for this evolutionary concept. Acceptance of how we are evolving in consciousness as a human race relieves society of many of the fear-based rules and regulations that it enforces, often by restrictions and war. Along with a change in attitude towards same sex marriage and our understanding of trans-gender people we need a change in how death is perceived.

Everyone has a story, and when a person takes responsibility for their story they grow their soul by becoming more aware and conscious of how their thoughts, words, and deeds affect themselves and others. Every thought and feeling has a vibration that has the potential to calm and reassure or to worsen a situation. This is evident at the bedside of a person who is dying, and an example of how professional caregivers can influence the wished-for state of peace. Human beings are more than the role they play or title and position they may hold. One of my early patients who was dying at home defined her role as the provider of family meals. When she was able, she stored the meals she lovingly prepared in her freezer. When her husband told me that he had taken over that role, the patient visibly suffered the emotion of loss. For me, being useful and contributing to society as a whole is an emotional need that will play a part in my decision to give myself up to the process of dying.

When facing death, a person seems compelled to put their affairs in order or attend to unfinished business. This process involves healing relationships that could have ended differently, accepting the consequences of choices and paths not taken, releasing feelings that could have been different – not seeking to hurt or to make guilty - and letting go of old emotional burdens with forgiveness of self and others. "Dying before you die" is one way of saying "to live each day as if it was our last" and is a beneficial spiritual exercise. Spirituality is a more individual matter than religion, it does not rely on an external organisation; however, comforting and nurturing membership of an organisation can be. Spirituality is an experience of the inner life. It is universal and mystical in that one can sense a direct experience of the "super computer." It transcends race, ethnic groups, culture, and tradition. It is the capacity to explore the inner self - the "I am."

Once birthed into this mortal form, we have no recollection of our former life, and need to rediscover who we are over and over again, with the aim of gaining insights into karmic forces, awareness, or greater consciousness of a co-creative process with our Maker or the Beloved. Different religions and beliefs have different names for what is commonly known as God. Enlightenment is recognised as a process of discovering the world within. The internal self is where the dream world can be thought of as an interface between this reality and the next. Those who have an active dream life are less likely to fear the transition from being to non-being. Going within is achieved with a spiritual practice such as meditation in its many forms and learning to listen to the voice of intuition, as well as recognising the unconscious and collective unconscious. The mind thinks in images; an example of this for those who are influenced by the Buddhist tradition is the image of a smiling serene Buddha.

The barrier between the level of consciousness achieved in this realm and the consciousness of the One Consciousness (God) is referred to as "the veil." People who are near to death frequently refer to seeing light, which is another metaphor for what cannot be experienced fully until the veil is lifted. Physicians of all callings, the world over, will have their own perceptions of God and end of life responsibilities. The therapeutic relationship between the doctor and the patient needs to be one of mutual non-hierarchical respect. This is not something that can be legislated by a parliamentary vote. A vote in favor of physician-assisted dying may, however, encourage individuals to begin conversations about the mystery of death and how they view their life and their unique purpose. Such a vote, if successful, could be in danger of being choked with illusory safeguards. We live with a lack of security and uncertainty and, perhaps, rather than legislation, we need to explore what it is to have faith in a soul's purpose.

For thirty years, I worked at the bedside of people who were dying or in the process of parting the veil. I was privileged to be a private palliative care nurse and, with a private income, could walk this journey with those in my care by responding to their choices, beliefs, and values in a way that gave the person a sense of their place in the larger scheme of world views. This required integrity and a sound knowledge of the principles and practice of palliative care, and what was legal and what was not. Being in the presence of death is a learning experience like no other. A healing relationship with a person who is dying needs to be authentic and real. The care giver needs to be self-aware; we take ourselves to our work, which means that our gifts and imperfections are on show. In this book, I am sharing some of the insights I have gained into what is commonly called "a good death."

As with many family businesses, my NurseLink family of nurses and care givers went the second mile in their work of supporting people at the end of their life. In return, they were rewarded not only financially, but also with great insights into this most important phase of life. A scale of professional charges, which included a respite rate, was introduced, so that we could continue with the work that we grew to love. The care we gave was person-centred and flexible rather than governed by industrial rules and regulations. This was highlighted when one nurse was caring for a dying woman who had chosen to spend her last days by the sea. The large window that looked out at the sea was cloudy with sea spray, and the patient asked the nurse if she would clean it for her so that she could see the sea more clearly. The registered nurse contacted me and asked if this task was included in the care plan? I said that if it raises the energy levels of the patient, we clean the window, and that it that was not a difficult task as the window was at ground level. Spending time with the patient and being there as needed was far more satisfying for both parties. The alternative offered by some organisations was to provide quick in and out visits, which made performing tasks a priority. These may or may not have been timely. It is difficult to time needs such as toileting, reaching for an object or being woken to answer the door. My nursing standard was to be personal, flexible, and centred on the holistic needs of the patient. In many cases, this meant long hours at the bedside. Being there - just being ready to respond as the need arises.

When industry bodies enforced standard award rates of pay and conditions, the type of care that NurseLink was able to provide, for three decades, ceased. Dying at home was no longer possible for many, as the costs became prohibitive. Accepting support was difficult for many of my private sector patients as pride and a sense of self-determination was strong. This is also my nature. I, too, needed to let go of control and bow down to what was evolving. End of life is a time when nurses are highly valued. Not only do they understand the procedures for giving medication, they are accepted as a pair of hands to look after the body as it declines and poses daily challenges. Florence Nightingale, the founder of modern nursing, had a vision for nurses, which is relevant in today's world. She recognised the importance of considering feelings, attending to hygiene and recognising nature's laws that put the patient in the best possible environment for natural healing to take place. She also overcame the restrictions of systems and the prejudices of individuals.

End of life is a time in a person's life like no other, and deserves a personal, flexible, creative and intuitive approach. It is about the transition of the soul, and responds to forces of love, compassion, and the freedom to be oneself. Knowledge of integrative medicine and a broad spectrum of care, as well as paper qualifications, may reduce the need for costly industry accreditation. As one surgeon wrote in his memoir, "Human warmth is more comforting than pethidine (an opioid medication)." The Golden Rule, "do unto others as you would have them do unto you," is a goal worth striving for in end-of-life care. In my case, this means that I would like to be cared for in a way that puts me in charge and meets my needs, as I see them as much as possible. It means having a peaceful environment staffed with enlightened beings - from this world and the next.

CHAPTER 1

Dying with Confidence

My primary tasks as a palliative care nurse were to empower people to die with confidence and to support their families in their bereavement. People approached death in various ways. I identified the following as people who died with confidence:

1. A person who has had a near-death experience or a connection with a person after their physical death.
2. A person who follows a religion that gives life meaning and purpose. "The lamps are different—the light is the same" (Rumi).
3. A person who follows a spiritual path other than an organised religion, and perhaps has a deep knowing and dream life that intuits that it is their time. "We are spiritual beings immersed in a human experience" (Teilhard de Chardin).
4. A person who has faith in their doctor, hospice, nurse or other decision maker to make decisions in their best interest - requiring trust and truthfulness
5. A person who has taken comfort from the experiences of others in the books they have written. To mention a few: *Proof of Heaven: a Neurosurgeon's Journey into the Afterlife* by Eben Alexander MD; *Life Between Lives: Many Lives, Many Masters* by Brian L Weiss MD; *Visions, Trips, and Crowded Rooms: Who and What You See Before You Die* by David Kessler;
6. A person who holds a firm belief that death is the end of everything - dust to dust! There is no eternal soul.

REFLECTING ON A PERSON WHO HAS HAD A NEAR-DEATH EXPERIENCE OR CONNECTION WITH A PERSON AFTER THEIR PHYSICAL DEATH

I have been privileged to have had both. At the age of forty, I had my own near-death experience when I continued to hemorrhage following a vaginal hysterectomy. I had been discharged from hospital and driven home by the good woman who was minding my children. My husband was at work. As I stepped out of the car, I experienced blood pouring down my legs. I phoned my husband to contact the hospital to arrange for my readmission. I felt that my life force was leaving me along with the bright-red blood. I was readmitted. The foot of my bed was raised and concerned nurses tried to measure my blood pressure. I was told that I would need to go back to theatre. At that time, I felt extraordinary peace and knew that I had tried to be a good wife and mother, and that my children were all healthy and intelligent and that someone would take care of them. The peace I experienced was profound. In fact, I was surprised when I woke up from the anesthetic! While my convalescent period was lengthy, I recovered and never feared death again.

I have fond memories of Henry, who I cared for two decades ago. He had been a very successful builder who rejected care in the local hospice and chose my home-based palliative care service. It was not an easy case, but Henry got his wish to die at home. Before he died, my nurses accompanied him in his Rolls Royce for a weekend in his holiday house on a local river. Whatever he wanted in these last days of life was facilitated by his family and my nurses. A week after he died, I was awoken by the smell of cigarette smoke. This was strange because no one smoked in my home. I dismissed the thought and fell back into sleep. It happened again the next night. This time, I recognised the smell. It was the smell of Henry's cigarettes. I sat up in bed and thought, *OK, Henry, what do you want to tell me?* The message was clear.

Henry told me to be more businesslike and to look after his granddaughter. As if by synchronicity, his granddaughter came into the office looking for work the very next day. She was a medical student, and worked with my patients for some time as a palliative care assistant. I had forgotten about this incident until twenty-five years later when I met a member of his family at a social function. She reminded me that her grandfather had made the choice to spend his last days at home. I mention Henry to reinforce the fact that the unseen world exists and has the power to influence our life in physical form. David Kessler, a renowned co-author with Elisabeth Kubler-Ross on death and grief, in his book *Visions, Trips and Crowded Rooms: Who and What You See Before You Die,* writes about the miraculous encounters and deathbed phenomenon he and others have witnessed. These stories are many, and perhaps need to be normalised more often in end of life education.

The following quotes come from *Amazing Encounters: Direct Communication from the Afterlife,* a book written by Elizabeth Keane, PhD.

> The unexpected appearance or presence of a loved one who has died can be a heart-stopping shock for a person in the midst of grief

> Some believe they are grief-induced hallucinations – yet people remembered their encounters very clearly, even after a long time

> We are all part of a greater reality – and those who have had these experiences have been blessed to touch and be touched by this greater reality

> Life was not the same ever again

Another book which I found comforting was written by Cherie Sutherland PhD. The book is entitled *Transformed by the Light: life after near death experiences.*

> They were recognised by bodily vision, dreams, synchronicities in the experiences, recognition of presence, "I felt very strongly that God was there in my life", hearing voices and feelings

> Going through a tunnel towards intense light to a wondrous sense of peace

Life takes on a different face and there is a drastic change in priorities and a more developed sense of purpose following a near death experience

Looking at new grandson: "I felt a touch of my grandfather coming through…" Reincarnation became real.

REFLECTING ON A PERSON WHO FOLLOWS A RELIGION

"The lamps are different—the light is the same" - Rumi

I give examples of people who have found comfort from a religion in Chapter Five. In some cases, it seemed that the teachings learned in childhood came back to offer comfort. In others, early teachings, particularly of hellfire and judgement, came back to frighten and confuse.

The five most influential religions of the world are Buddhism, Christianity, Hinduism, Islam, and Judaism. While all religions have their dark side and have the potential to divide rather than bring together, they provide a visible institutional form of God in society. They form the focus for valuable community-building and encourage rituals. Many a landscape is dotted with beautiful churches, temples, and other places of worship. However, while individual inward-looking spirituality can be found in a religion, it is evident that many people turn to non-institutional expressions of spirituality. In the funeral service, there is a tendency to replace religious leaders with celebrants, and visits to the bedside of person who is dying person are more often made by a pastoral care worker.

I have tried to find the common threads that run through all religions and to research the religion that was giving comfort to my patients. While I refer to myself as an agnostic Buddhist Catholic who recites Hindu mantras and had a Methodist upbringing, it has been my association with the Catholic church that taught me my first steps towards self-knowledge and consciousness. One nun friend used to say, "Joy, the mind is like a parachute, it functions best when fully open!"

Andrew Harvey, who is a scholar, author, and teacher of mystical traditions, and co-editor of Sogyal Rinpoche's book *The Tibetan Way of*

Living and Dying, says that Buddha gave teachings for the mind while Jesus gave teachings for the heart. While Jesus taught to love one another and to do unto others as they would do unto you, Buddha taught that suffering ceases when attachment to desire ceases. The Buddhist Eight-Fold path is a guide for living:

1. Right Understanding
2. Right Thought
3. Right Speech
4. Right Action
5. Right Livelihood
6. Right Effort
7. Right Mindfulness
8. Right Concentration

Buddhism is a religion and a philosophy that encompasses a variety of traditions, beliefs and spiritual practices, largely based on original teachings attributed to the Buddha and resulting interpreted philosophies. To die with confidence, a Buddhist philosophy teaches that the person needs to die free of attachments. What might people become attached to?

- Beliefs, habits, and associations that may or may not serve them
- A desired persona—youthful, beautiful, sporty, pious, trendy
- A trauma. Sense of injustice or other emotional wound
- Possessions and worldly gains. Power and titles
- An egoic sense of self, things we identify with, such as a car, club membership, school, and role or profession in life
- A standing in society
- This known world!

REFLECTING ON A PERSON WHO FOLLOWS A SPIRITUAL PATH OTHER THAN RELIGION

The following wisdom on spirituality comes from Emeritus Professor Ian Maddocks, AM:

> A principal component of spirituality, a sense of belonging, being not alone, being in touch with something greater than self. May be found in religion, in nature, in music, in art; is closely related to love. Can lead to serenity, a preparedness for whatever is to come.

This person may be one who has a mystical view of the world and connects with a natural world order such as shamanism. It may be someone who has esoteric beliefs and follows a Hierarchy of Masters. For many people, a faith in God gives way to an experiential discovery of the soul deep within and its journey over many lifetimes. Alice Bailey was one of the first writers to use the term "New Age." Her works, written between 1919 and 1949, describe a wide-ranging system of esoteric thought, covering such topics as how spirituality relates to the solar system, meditation, healing, spiritual psychology, and the destiny of nations. These writings were known as "Ageless Wisdom." Her vision of a unified society included a global spirit of religion. The Tibetan Master, Sogyal Rinpoche, talks about believing in the concept of God while believing in the skyline spaciousness of nature mind. Others find their sense of spirituality in the Goddess movement.

Another author to make an impact on people's beliefs was James Redfield, the author of *The Celestine Prophecy*. In this book, the concept of humans as energetic vibrations is posed—the higher vibration is an indication of the soul's evolution. "The Ninth Insight" suggested that beauty and finding one's path increased energy vibrations to reveal a portal between heaven and earth. Fear lowered the energy vibrations and closed the veil. Each culture tries to define the mystery of life and death. It seems that the human collective mind is a mystery and contains much illusion, and God is perceived with marvelous diversity. The Sufi mystic Rumi says:

> *Make everything in you an ear, each atom of your being, and you will hear at every moment what the Source is whispering to you, just to you and you, without any need for my words or anyone else's.*

This is sound advice for a person who is on the highway of life and sees an exit sign in the distance, and knows that this is the point at which to leave the highway. This whispering from the Source, if trusted, can enable the soul in the physical vehicle to exit with confidence. I was asked by a caring son to look after his mother, who wished to stay at home in spite of her dementia. Accepting care is difficult when the rational mind is chaotic, but, strangely, this elderly woman accepted my professional nursing support and told me that she was not afraid to die because, one day, she had been in a church and heard a voice telling her that she would be looked after. Her care continued for several years until she fell in the bathroom. Hospitalisation followed and much to her horror, she was discharged to the place she had fiercely resisted: a nursing home. She was only there a day when she told her sister that her husband, who had long since left this earth, would come for her after lunch the next day. He did! She died at the precise moment that she had intuited.

Most of our lives are lived from our unconscious or deep inner reality. For a person to heal from unconscious emotional wounds, it may be necessary to seek guidance from a health practitioner who can identify and bring these wounds to consciousness. Once something is understood, it ceases to have a hold over the person. Triggers from childhood wounds such as harsh words spoken by a parent, outbursts of anger or unkind labels live on in the unconscious and have the potential to give false beliefs and limit achievements. The unconscious realm is known in meditation, altered states of consciousness, dreams, music, art, poetry, and what symbols and events push our buttons. For spiritual growth to occur, a person may evolve to recognise higher patterns of energy, which some call archetypes, gods, angels and spiritual guardians. It is about becoming self-aware through association with these patterns and character profiles.

Healing invisible wounds is a prerequisite for dying with confidence. People who do so have been able to reframe life events that have caused emotional pain and lacked meaning. A key to peace is forgiveness, which takes many forms. Forgiveness can be a kind word or action. An action may be to write what the heart wants to say or visualise the hurt rising in a hot air balloon to be blown away. Stories about people who have reframed their life include the soldier who lost his arm when a bomb exploded in a war zone becoming an inspiring hero by participating in the Invictus Games: these sporting games are international events for wounded armed services personnel. They were created and are supported by Prince Harry the Duke of Sussex. People who are held in high esteem have a role of leadership to perform.

Patrick Oliver, a former Catholic priest, author and spiritual director taught me much about personal awareness and the dream state. He uses the analogy of the tree to describe the parts of a person that can be seen and the parts of a person that cannot be seen, such as the root system. In this analogy, the root system represents a person's unconscious dimension. Roots can be damaged, starved of water and deprived of nourishment. If the fruit of the tree is withered it is not effective to pour nourishment on the fruit itself. Rather the nourishment needs to reach the roots so that the whole life of the fruit tree is healed. So it is with the human soul. The nourishment it needs to shine as a beacon in the world begins in the root system of early childhood. It is not effective when seeking the health of the body to administer medications alone, without looking at root causes.

A PERSON WHO HAS FAITH IN THEIR DOCTOR, HOSPICE, NURSE, OR SUBSTITUTE DECISION-MAKER TO MAKE DECISIONS IN THEIR BEST INTEREST

This requires trust and truthfulness. This allows people to pursue a wide range of options, which may include the traditional medical model as well as complementary therapies. Respect needs to be given for a person's beliefs and chosen lifestyle. In a presentation to the volunteers of Sandakan Hospice, in East Malaysia, I listed the following as being attributes to foster in the life of a hospice volunteer:

- Being positive rather than negative in one's attitude
- Being loving as opposed to hateful
- Being kind rather than cruel
- Being inclusive rather than exclusive
- Being generous rather than mean spirited
- Being knowledgeable rather than ignorant
- Being wise and not foolish
- Being respectful rather than disrespectful
- Being humble rather than self-important
- Wanting the best for others rather than feeling jealous

- Being strong rather than weak
- Seeking peace rather than war and disagreements

There are many lessons to be learned from the pioneers of the Hospice Movement. Dame Cicely Saunders, the founder of this way of caring for people at the end of their life, confirmed that how people die remains in the memory of those who live on. I found that if a person had experienced a less-than-favourable death, the memory remained with the grieving family and friends long after the death. The memory may become associated with the place of death, who was present, the manner of death, or who was deemed to be in charge. A new way of experiencing death was what I offered in my nurse practice. To do this, I first needed to confront my own beliefs about death and dying, and what I was attached to or avoided.

Dame Cicely Saunders was a remarkable woman who trained as a nurse before training as a social worker and doctor. I particularly related to her life when she was advised to train as a doctor because no one would listen to her as a nurse. Florence Nightingale had much the same experience with doctors in the Crimean war. There, many difficulties were thrown in her way. She overcame them by inventing the pie chart to demonstrate in statistical terms the results of her work. She was made a fellow of the Royal Statistical Society in recognition of her work. Dame Cicely Saunders is known as a deeply Christian person, and for her new methods of pain control. She had a revelation: "I realised that we needed not only better pain control but better overall care. People needed the space to be themselves." She coined the phrase "total pain." This included physical pain, bureaucratic bungling, visitors who did not visit, unfulfilled dreams and grief. I remember hearing her speak when I visited St. Christopher's Hospice in London in 1994 as part of a two week Hospice and Palliative Care Study Seminar in Great Britain. This study was organised by the US-based Hospice Education Institute. In her speech, she talked about the emotional pain experienced by one of her patients whose wife had to catch two buses to visit him.

Her concept of pain relief included emotional pain as well as physical pain. She said: "You matter because you are you, and you matter to the end of your life. We will do all we can not only to help you die peacefully, but also to live until you die." I like to think of peace as being a non-dual state where there is no right or wrong, black or white—just calm. The discipline of palliative care has progressed widely since the 1960s when Dame Cicely Saunders opened St. Christopher's Hospice. In many parts of the world it is a core subject for medical and nursing students, and assists people to die with confidence.

In this model, it is usually the doctor's responsibility to break the news that a cure for the body is no longer an option and that a palliative care approach needs to be introduced. Cultural and other considerations need to be observed when breaking news of a life-threatening diagnosis. Information can be given at a pace and manner that avoids misunderstanding or misinterpretation. How much information is given, and to whom, will differ from case to case. When there are many attachments to life, loved ones, fame and fortune, the person is more vulnerable to pain and suffering when they receive a terminal diagnosis. Elisabeth Kubler-Ross would say that people with cancer are the lucky ones, for they usually have time to put their affairs in order. Mystical principles teach that when attachments are not released the karmic energy carries them into the next lifetime.

Palliative care has been described as an approach that improves the quality of life, rather than the quantity of life, for patients and their families facing the problems associated with a terminal illness, through the prevention and relief of suffering. It requires impeccable assessment and treatment of all pain that is associated with the physical, emotional and spiritual aspects of the person. This approach incorporates an accepting attitude towards death as a part of life, and requires all service providers to work together in a person-centred way. It respects the wishes of the elderly in relation to the medications that can be ceased if their purpose is not focussed on comfort and encourages everyone to make an Advance Care Directive. All patients have a right to refuse treatment that may be futile in the face of their disease.

BOOKS THAT REASSURE AND GIVE CONFIDENCE

One day I was asked to visit a man who had been returned home from hospital to die. His brother was with him as I introduced myself and inquired after his overall health and daily routines. In the course of this conversation, I mentioned the book *Proof of Heaven: A Neurosurgeon's Journey into the Afterlife* by Eben Alexander, MD. As it happened, I had a copy with me, and had recently read it with enthusiasm. While there are many books on this theme, I felt the fact that this book was written by a doctor gave it a different perspective. I shared my thoughts about life after death with the patient and his brother. In the conversation that followed, this man's brother provided me with the highlights, as well as outlining the difficult times, of the patient's life. It was a valuable reflective time. There seemed no hurry to leave this world so I was surprised to learn that he had died in peace the next day. The book, it seemed to me, was the medicine that gave this man comfort and the will to cease the battle to stay alive when his body was so obviously crumbling. A case of belief structuring reality.

Traditionally, holy books, poetry, and chants have given comfort. In this fast-paced world, people look for inspiration that gives them the capacity to be themselves and to make up their own minds about why we are here. They appreciate reassurance from fellow travellers that death is not the end and that there is a future of a different kind in an unseen world. Cutting through life's many illusions has been likened to peeling an onion layer by layer to reach the core. People are evolving in the same way the universe is evolving. Another way of saying this is that we are all co-creators with the "super computer" if we choose. Much anguish is felt by people who resist change. Those who have stopped clinging to the known and who embrace change are more likely to appreciate books that are written today, in addition to those writings whose "wisdom words" live on and continue to energise today.

REFLECTING ON THOSE WITH A DISBELIEF IN GOD AND A SOUL'S JOURNEY

No matter how many answers I think I may have to the transition phase of life, this attitude to life and death I find puzzling. Puzzling because the people who have expressed this belief have appeared to be just as happy and content as people who have a spiritual belief in life after death. Elisabeth Kubler-Ross wrote widely on the needs of the dying. These needs included non-judgmental, unconditional love. The love that says I respect your beliefs, which may be different to mine because we are complex creations and our small minds find meaning in our unique personalities.

Not everyone wants to live in a box. Intellect alone is a very limited tool with which to discover the paradoxical nature of existence. Also, I am aware that what is expressed in one level of consciousness is a different reality in another deeper level of consciousness. This was demonstrated to me while talking with an elderly woman who had experienced a heart attack. When she recovered, she was discharged from hospital to her home, where we met. She protested strongly that she should have been allowed to die and not resuscitated. I informed her that she had the opportunity to document her wishes. Then, I produced a form called The Natural Death Act (now replaced with an Advance Care Directive). Strangely, she was adamant about not signing the form.

Whatever one's conscious beliefs, it may be helpful to consider a short life review and contemplate the following:

> These things I have loved in life…
> These experiences I have cherished…
> These beliefs I have outgrown…
> These ideas have liberated me…
> These convictions I have lived by…
> These insights I have arrived at…
> These risks I have taken…
> These things I have lived for…
> These sufferings have had silver linings…
> Life has taught me these lessons…
> These people have shaped my life…
> These holy readings have helped me…
> These things I regret about my life…
> These are my life's achievements…
> These persons are enshrined in my heart…
> These are my unfulfilled desires…

It is not difficult to appreciate that people come to different conclusions about life on earth and one's purpose and meaning influenced by their personality, experiences, and training. Iain McGilchrist, author of *The Master and His Emissary* argues that the two halves of the brain have different functions. The right hemisphere is open, patient, empathetic, more interested in process than results. The left hemisphere sees detail, is precise, with an objective narrow focus. When working together, they give clarity and precision, plus intuition and faith. They combine science and the arts, and give facts and metaphor.

Perhaps, a disbelief in a life after death can be a way of just being in the Now without distracting thoughts and feelings. This state of presence is what meditators strive to achieve.

CHAPTER 2

My Beginnings

The most important wisdom tip for me to share came from a dream: I was in a war zone and trapped in a lower level basement with a dusty concrete floor. I could hear the noise of planes and intuitively knew their intent was to completely demolish the building I was in. I knew that I was going to die by suffocation or by getting crushed with more falling concrete slabs. I calmly brushed the dust away from where I rested my nostrils and as I did so reminded myself to keep love in my heart as I prepared for death. I was at peace. "Keep love in your heart" was a mantra I would encourage patients to say as they concentrated on their last breaths.

> Your light burned away my last illusion
> The world and I died together
> I woke a ghost smiling among ghosts
> Unreal and gentle in a world of you
>
> —Rumi

Dying with confidence is assisted by giving confident nursing care. In my holistic model of care, a person's needs are considered in four areas of their life, with each quadrant needing equal attention: all are interrelated. A symptom felt in the body will have a connection to the other areas. For example, sweaty palms and a dry mouth may be an indication of nervousness. Emotions are felt in the body and understood in the intellect. It is instinctual for a person in a fearful situation to pray to God or seek a mother's protection. Esoteric philosophy considers a personality to include the physical body, the mental body, and the emotional body. The body tells the story of a person's life.

This book is concerned with questions such as:

- Did my life have a deeper meaning?
- Did I have a purpose to fulfill?
- How did my soul travel in the journey of life?
- Am I a better person for having lived?
- Did I fulfill my potential?
- What did I contribute to others (e.g., family, friends, God)?
- What is my "unfinished business"?
- What acts can I do to resolve past hurts?
- What lifts my spirit?
- How do I prepare for the next life?
- What supports a life lived by faith rather than fear?

A lack of spiritual energy may be experienced as:

- Feeling hollow inside and powerless
- Feeling worthless, anxious, uncertain, excluded from friends and family
- Experiencing the 'dark night of the soul' – beliefs that helped previously no longer comfort
- Lacking in self-esteem, self-awareness – needing support and compassion from others
- Experiencing disturbing dreams and buried memories rising from the unconscious.

ETHICAL CONSIDERATIONS FOR A GOOD DEATH

Scottish Palliative Care pioneer, Dr. Derek Doyle says that palliative care is about three things: the quality of life, the value of life and the meaning of life.

Ethics are not as precise as legal requirements and often require deliberation by an ethics committee. They are a guidance system for end-of-life care and include:

Four Principles
Respecting individual rights
Doing no harm
Doing good
Being fair

Four Rules
Keeping promises
Telling the truth
Keeping secrets
Maintaining dignity

One family highlighted "Doing no harm" when they wanted to perform a symbolic cultural ritual. This was to lay ceremonial clothes on the body of the person who was near death. There were many times when I was asked to promise to be present at the time of death or to attend a special celebration. My life was unpredictable and I was seldom in a position to give reassurance that I would be present at the time of death. I used to say, jokingly, that if my physical presence was required, the gods need to time your departure for when I am available. Some family disclosures were difficult to keep, and I needed a trusted, more experienced person to unburden my anxiety. Telling the truth is difficult, especially when the patient is cognitively impaired in a case of dementia. It is interesting to note that such patients seemed to know what words were true or false. Rightly or wrongly, I would resort to giving answers as if responding to feelings, and avoid using a factual language. Maintaining dignity was always a goal. However, there were times when a person suffering from dementia acted with a lack of former dignity—almost as an unlived life being let out of a cage.

The soul of a person always needed to be considered. My first prayer I remember as a child still in a cot was about soul: "Now I lay me down to sleep I pray thee Lord my soul to keep – if I should die before I wake I pray the Lord my soul to take."

Sogyal Rinpoche, the Tibetan Buddhist author, writes that one of the chief reasons we have so much anguish and difficulty facing death is that we ignore the truth of impermanence. We desperately want everything to continue as it is. Another view is put forward by modern-day mystic Thomas Hubl. He suggests that fear at the time of death may not be related to death but rather to the anguish experienced from the realising that time for fulfilling a life's purpose and making acts to heal relationships were running out. Trauma in the past affects us today. Thomas Hubl refers to a person's emotional landscape where a person gets to know love, joy, sadness, anger, and guilt. He also refers to the rational self, where patterns, understandings, and new ways of thinking, such as trusting intuition, become part of life.

I particularly relate to the story of the Buddhist student who went to his master and asked the master to teach him about death. The master said that the student must first learn about life. So the student asked the master to teach him about life. The master replied that to do that was to learn about death, for they are one. Wisdom and grace directs a person to see through illusions and to evolve. I view soul as a bus terminal, where a personality gets off one bus and onto a new bus and a new physical experience through reincarnation.

My prompting for writing this book follows on from the interest in my books *As Good As Goodbyes Get: A Window into Death and Dying* and *My Way: One Nurse's Passion for End of Life.* In those books, I wrote about the people I had nursed in my capacity as a private palliative care nurse specialising in personalised end-of-life care and about my personal and professional soul journey experiences. It has been my experience that fear of seeing death as an unwelcome threshold is one of the reasons why people fail to prepare for this transition from one state of being to another. I sometimes imagine that the elderly who are in nursing homes could be given the choice of a medication to induce sleep or a personal device such as an iPad playing meditative music. In writing this book, it is my intention to encourage conversations of this important life event and to reclaim some of the ground that has been lost by outsourcing end-of-life entirely to others.

Until I was forty-eight I had been the wife of a successful orthodontist, raising four children, who today have careers and children of their own. My first child, a son, was born in London, and as a result of pre-eclampsia, mother and baby nearly died. That was my first near-death experience. My second child, a girl, was born in Rochester, New York State. Two more boys were born when my husband and I returned to Australia. We were married in London. Following a ceremony in a Catholic church vows were heard by a registrar in the church office. It seemed like we were being married twice. However, these ceremonies did not secure the marriage and we divorced in 1992. It was an era when the role of married women was primarily to support the breadwinner, be a home-maker, and to raise the children. My mentor, Florence Nightingale, railed against marriage and wrote that if a woman was to pursue her own interests, this had to be done in odd moments. She asked if Michelangelo could have painted the Sistine Chapel at odd moments! When my youngest child was nearing the end of his secondary education I returned to nursing; the career I left to marry.

Before returning to nursing, my life was occupied with children, working part-time in my husband's orthodontic practice, and playing bridge and golf. It was also an exciting time when computers were introduced. My home computer was mainly used for accounting, word-processing children's university assignments, and Christmas correspondence. My husband bought me my first mobile phone, and this rather heavy device caused much interest on the golf course. In spite of a seemingly idyllic life, I was restless and slow to listen to the voice of intuition, which was prodding me to change my way of life.

When I did listen, I enrolled in a refresher course in nursing at the Royal Brisbane Hospital, and worked part-time in the Mary Potter Hospice in North Adelaide. This hospice was run by The Little Company of Mary and in the tradition of their founder, Mother Mary Potter. This was a time when the philosophy of hospice care was becoming established as a better way to care for patients who were dying, mainly from cancer. I loved the work and had an immediate connection with Mary Potter, whose life was one of struggle and persistence. Her ideal was that the dying should be cared for with a mother's love. As a mother, I related to this ideal.

Following my time at the Mary Potter Hospice, I felt driven to begin my own private nurse practice. I was frustrated by not having the time to connect with patients at a deeper level in the hospice. I was interested in their emotional and spiritual needs as well as their physical needs. It was particularly frustrating to come on duty to find the bed of a patient empty and be expected to carry on with a "new day" attitude. I wanted more. In 1987, another hospice nurse, Susan Forth, and I formed a company called Private Palliative Care Services Pty Ltd and began the difficult task of promoting a private nurse practice, offering home-based palliative care.

It could have been the last straw for our marriage to be on twenty-four-hour call for seven days via a pager system. The family had to share my time, yet I knew in the depths of my soul that this was my calling. It became my passion. I remember one patient who managed to celebrate her 100th birthday. She tested my commitment when she paged me at four in the morning because she had accidently emptied a glass of water in her bed and wanted the bed changed. I went. After this test, we shared a close and trusting relationship. She much preferred an indwelling urinary drainage catheter to the tiresome effort required to use a bed pan or to getting out of bed to use a commode chair. She enjoyed occlusive dressings that needed less changing to protect the parts of her body that were vulnerable to damage from pressure. The daily bed sponge was a performance that resembled a surgical procedure. That is one of the stories I wrote about in *As Good As Goodbyes Get: A Window into Death and Dying.* I learned early that for nursing support to be valued, it had to be flexible and person-centred rather than service-centred.

Having gained my initial qualifications as a registered nurse at the Princess Alexandra Hospital in South Brisbane, I travelled to Canada where I worked in St. Joseph's Hospital, Toronto, before continuing on to the Simpson Memorial Maternity Hospital in Edinburgh, Scotland, for midwifery training. My training in Brisbane was when nurses lived in the nurses' home and worked split shifts and long hours in the wards for very little money. It was a matter of learning on the job and taking responsibility at a very young age. It was also a time when nurses sacrificed the health of their backs in providing patient care.

Following weeks of intensive class room preliminary training we were ready for duty in the wards. That was an exciting, albeit daunting, time. Training continued by way of lectures given by tutor sisters and medical consultants as well as ward experience. In retrospect, a junior nurse spent much time counting cutlery, boiling bed pans, straightening the wheels of the beds to be in a uniform line, stacking and counting linen and, worst of all, emptying sputum mugs from patients suffering from lung diseases. It took four years to gain the qualification of registered nurse. Those close to me, who recognised my duchess archetype, were surprised that I completed this arduous training. It was to become my ticket to travel the world in search of experiences and knowledge.

After graduation, another nurse friend and I boarded a ship in Sydney and set sail for Canada. We had a return ticket and very little else by way of worldly goods. We shared a six-berth cabin in one of the lower decks, as it was the cheapest. As it happened, the first class passengers were short of young and exciting girls so we were frequently invited to take part in activities on the upper decks. I believe I had a guardian angel looking after me, and my innocence saved me from situations of danger. I just did not know what the cabin boy was talking about when, with a wink, he offered me an empty cabin.

The then love of my life was studying at Stanford University, and although we needed to land in Vancouver to fulfill immigration requirements, the ship went to San Francisco for no extra cost. This was an obstacle to overcome, and I was driven to find a way around the dilemma of a free voyage to San Francisco and fulfilling the requirements to be a landed Canadian immigrant. It was when Senator John Kennedy had just been elected as president of the United States. I found an address and wrote him a letter of congratulations. I also outlined the frustration we were experiencing with not being permitted to continue the voyage to San Francisco. I received a polite reply that said nothing about a solution but, perhaps by coincidence, permission was granted. Where there is a will there is a way! Looking back, I cannot believe the absence of fear in a twenty-two year old so far from home. It never occurred to me to take out travel insurance. I do remember making a will and leaving it with my parents' solicitor.

Toronto was chosen for a working destination when a map of Canada was laid out on the floor and one of us put a pin in the map while blindfolded. The hospital was chosen by examining the list of hospitals and the names of the matrons. St. Joseph's Hospital in Toronto had a nun in charge called Sister Matilda. We were attracted to Matilda because of the connection with the popular Australian song "Waltzing Matilda." There was a unified 'yes' and applications were sent. The hospital had more generous working conditions than the one in Australia. We enjoyed it so much so that we would work for a private nursing agency on our days off. I particularly liked the system of total care for our allocated patients.

I was used to a hierarchy of nursing responsibilities, from juniors emptying bed pans to senior nurses doing ward rounds with doctors. In St. Joseph's, I related to the practice of one nurse giving a patient total care. For example, the same nurse in charge gave diuretics to increase the volume of urine *and* recorded the result. As a junior nurse, I knew there were times when I forgot to measure the contents of the bedpan before discarding the contents in the sluice because the need had not been reinforced by the giving of the medication. I liked the way a nurse could order laboratory tests if a urinary infection was suspected and have the results to show the doctor, instead of waiting for the doctor to visit before ordering the test. I also remember having to drop to our knees in the corridor when the ringing of a bell heralded the priest passing by with Holy Communion. Times have changed.

After working in Canada and completing Part 1 midwifery in Edinburgh, Scotland, I worked as a private nurse in London. Working for an agency gave me flexibility in my work and I was able to take travel breaks. I was privileged to be welcomed into a range of homes from the very wealthy to the working class. My interest was how people lived, what they valued, how they liked things done and how I could be an effective advocate for them. Watching my first birth at the Simpson Memorial Pavilion in Edinburgh was awe inspiring. This was a time when the father of the baby was not encouraged to be at the birth, and soon after birth the young mother broke the news herself to the father via the telephone that had been wheeled to the bedside.

Student midwives worked long hours and for very little pay. There were three Australian nurses on our preliminary training course and we were keen to explore Scotland. On occasions, we would hire a small car and set off exploring from Edinburgh to Iona and from Edinburgh to Inverness. We enjoyed the contrasts of heather covered fields where sheep grazed to the peaceful vistas of Loch Lomond and Loch Ness. Stern Tutor Sisters reminded us that we were there to study midwifery not to see the countryside. My name at that time was McClintock, so I felt close to my Scottish heritage. The time spent in training covered Christmas and New Year. As if on cue, it snowed for Hogmanay, the Scottish celebrations signifying the end of the old year and the beginning of the new. Christmas was an ordinary working day.

Reflecting on heritage, my parents were good people whose own parents were pioneers in the new country of Australia having arrived from England, Scotland, and Ireland. Both of my grandfathers worked hard in the fledgling pineapple industry. My mother's father was given the title of "the pineapple king" in a framed picture that was hung in train carriages. My father's father began, what I believe to be, the first Australian pineapple cannery on his property. All seemed to have a respect for the church and my parents fervently progressed the Methodist church in adjacent districts. As an only and much-wanted girl, my wishes were indulged. My name "Joy" said it all for them. I had two older brothers. Sadly, my mother's first baby, a girl, had died at birth. My eldest brother had rheumatic fever before the era of penicillin and was in hospital for nearly a year. While bedbound, he made furniture for dolls using empty match boxes covered with colored felt fabric, and with cupboard doors and drawers that had beads for handles. The brother nearest my age encouraged me to play cricket and to climb trees. It was my wish to go to the city and to boarding school when I had completed primary school at a one teacher country school. There, I met many girls from different parts of the country and various walks of life. Many friends from those years are still friends.

The boarding school was small and was the same one that my mother had attended. She wanted me to learn music. I was a dismal failure at this activity. My mother played the organ at church and at home. As a special treat she would play "Over the Waves" by J. Rosas to induce a peaceful state and subsequent sleep. No wonder I used music in my nursing care and appreciated its therapeutic effects. The headmistress of my boarding school was to become a valuable mentor and did much to hone my character during those precarious adolescent years. On Sunday nights she gave talks to us on life skills. These included etiquette, understanding the changing physiology of our bodies, and issues that had arisen during the week. She took the older students to funerals and 'other' community activities to broaden our education. It was a five-hour steam train journey from my home to boarding school and then a long bus ride. I learned to make the journey alone. Travel and adventure seemed to be in my DNA even at an early age. Perhaps it's because I'm a Sagittarius.

This information is a backdrop to the following chapters, in which I share what life has taught me and the insights I have gained through my varied life experiences. I have always taught that we bring ourselves to work and our personality needs to have an uplifting effect on those in our care. My website, www.joynugent.com, gives praise to some of my many mentors.

CHAPTER 3

My Journey into Soul

> There is an almost sensual longing for communion with others who have a larger vision. The immense fulfillment of the friendships between those engaged in furthering the evolution of consciousness has a quality almost impossible to describe.
>
> —Pierre Teilhard de Chardin

Pierre Teilhard de Chardin was an idealist philosopher and Jesuit priest who touches the hearts of all who seek a larger and deeper vision of life and individual meaning and purpose. To be at the bedside of a dying person, as I was many times over in the course of three decades, is a profound experience. It is no coincidence that hospice workers derive immense fulfillment from being present at the transition of a soul into another phase of consciousness. Feelings at this time are difficult to describe. The word "awe" comes to mind. When a dying person and their family have no particular faith underpinning their lives, I would refer to the God question as Love and would ask the person to hold a memory of love in their mind and to breathe in a loving feeling. I would say that God in any language is Love. A rung to cling to while on the ladder between life and death is comforting. That rung comes in different forms. For some, it may be traditional religious faith, and, for others, it may be a belief in Universal Divine Energy or a Mind of God, to which we have a connection. My role was not to judge, or convert to my particular belief, but to be a conduit for what Florence Nightingale called "Universal Laws" while keeping my energy calm and loving.

The mental image of being a conduit for universal loving energy was taught at the various workshops on Therapeutic Touch I attended in Adelaide and in the USA. Therapeutic Touch is a contemporary way of channeling healing universal energy or performing "hands-on healing". The technique was perfected by Delores Krieger, PhD, RN, Professor Emeritus of Nursing at New York University, and Dora Kunz, a gifted energy healer who was able to describe visually a person's aura. In her book, *The Personal Aura*, Dora Kunz states that the chakras, or wheels of energy, are organs of consciousness and energy within the personal aura. She places the seven major centres at the crown of the head, brow, throat, heart, solar plexus, the genital region and the base of the spine. They serve as link between the personal energy fields, and distribute energy as it is needed for the many functions the body performs. I can strongly relate to the heart chakra opening up with an outpouring of energy when we feel love and compassion.

The *intention* to heal is of paramount importance for the person who is facilitating the healing. This person needs to be in a meditative and centred state of mind. The healing is not facilitated by the ego of the person performing the treatment. The "I" is merely the humble conduit holding an intention to be helpful. Without touching it, the hands hover five to ten centimeters over the body; *listening* to the person's energy field for sensory and intuitive cues which are felt in the palms of the hands. Energy medicine today is becoming more widely accepted. These cues may be sensations of hollowness, coldness, or heat, which the hands rhythmically clear and balance. One night, when I was preparing an elderly woman for bed, and with Therapeutic Touch in mind, I swept my hands from her head to her feet several times. She spontaneously remarked: "Joy, you are mesmerising me." What was it that she felt or sensed? My intention was to smooth away anything that would prevent a good night's sleep! There can be no emotional attachment to the outcome. The therapy is for the patient, not the healer.

One of my cases as a private nurse in London involved looking after a middle aged widow who was dying from cancer. Her only child, a daughter, who was my age at the time, was nursing her at home. I was forbidden to confirm to the mother that she had cancer and was, in fact, dying; I could only reassure her that the doctor was coming. It was an uncomfortable situation for all. There were no goodbyes, no expressions of trust in a life time principle, and no last instructions to guide and comfort the daughter. No wonder I grew to realise that supporting a person who is dying was so much more than pain relief for the physical body. In this case, personal power was abdicated to the doctor. I welcomed the early hospice movement, which I discovered several decades after this sad story.

My mother's death in 1979 was quite different. She died at home with her children present, and she had faith in a Methodist God to guide her. A great source of comfort, as she fought to stay strong, was a little cassette player, which played hymns day and night, sung in a Scottish accent. Music is the language of the soul. I felt that my mother's death was in total contrast to that earlier experience in London where there was no honest communication. It was my mother's death that led me to practice the holistic philosophy of palliative care. It was a time in my life when I was restless. I knew that I wanted more from life but did not know how or where to begin. It was a midlife crisis. My mother showed to me all the elements of a good death, as if she had a sacred contract to give me this experience. In *Sacred Contracts,* a book by intuitive healer Caroline Myss, I found the answer to the most frequently asked questions: "Why was I born? What is my sacred contract for this lifetime?" I intuitively knew that my restlessness was the catalyst for change.

Like my mentor Florence Nightingale, I learned from travel. Palliative Care Conferences took me to India, London, Montreal, Singapore, and East and West Malaysia. Conferences for Holistic Nurses took me from Adelaide to Sacramento and New York. For over ten years, I travelled to Sandakan, Sabah, in East Malaysia, with colleagues offering international education for doctors, nurses, and volunteers to the Sandakan Community-Based Hospice. These activities kept me updated with the traditional Western Medical model of palliative care practices, as well as providing an introduction to energy medicine. Allopathic medicine included learning about medications for symptom management and the various methods of their delivery. I regularly attended monthly Grand Rounds at the International Institute of Palliative & Supportive Studies in Adelaide. I invited leaders in their field to be presenters in the holistic education that was offered by NurseLink Foundation over a period of ten years.

NurseLink Foundation was founded in 2006 to extend the work of my holistic nursing practice. The objectives of the foundation were:

- To provide care and improve care for the aged and those with advanced illness or major disease;
- To promote the principles of health and palliative care as defined by the World Health Organisation for aged and community care;
- To foster and advocate an holistic and person-orientated approach to care. While supporting the physical and emotional needs of the individual, this approach also acknowledges each person's spiritual dimension and search for meaning, and values all traditional religions, faiths and cultures without favour.

An extensive library was shared with members of my caring team. Emotional pain and spiritual pain were not neglected. My aim was to build bridges between traditional Western medical care and Eastern influenced holistic care, the personality and the soul, and the soul and its cosmic source. Today, I coordinate monthly Soul Talks in South Australia. A primary object is to promote the prevention and treatment of death anxiety and the relevant symptoms of this mental disease, which may degenerate into death anxiety if left untreated. Four practitioners are invited to present on their professional work. One of the goals of the program is to honor and expand the work of health practitioners who are bringing a deeper perspective to their holistic complementary practices. Video recordings of these talks are made available on the Soul Talks' website, www.soultalks.com.au

The following poem by Rumi is a reminder of the need to recognise the personal barriers we all have to love, and fusing the personality of the lower self with the Higher Self or Soul. Rumi was a 13th-century Persian poet, Islamic scholar, and Sufi mystic whose spiritual legacy transcends national borders and ethnic divisions. Andrew Harvey called him the "Shakespeare of the Soul." I found it of interest that Rumi wrote over eighty poems on his love for Jesus. Once personal barriers are identified by making them conscious, the work of dissolving them can begin. There are many ways of gaining self-knowledge, and I share some of these in what follows.

> Your task is not to seek for love, but merely to seek and find all the barriers within yourself that you have built against it.

In preparation to work with people who were facing the end of their earthly life, I needed to know much more than the skills I learned as a registered general nurse. I needed to know the barriers within myself that would prevent me from giving the dying the unconditional non-judgemental love that Dr. Elisabeth Kubler-Ross taught. I attended one of her Life, Death, and Transition workshops in 1988. The workshop was held over a weekend in a scouts' camp in the beautiful Adelaide Hills. This workshop was the beginning of the long journey to self-discovery and the hidden traps and shadows buried in my unconscious. I first needed to recognise the many barriers that kept me from knowing my true self. I now understand it as a one-of-a-kind reflection of God's love in the world, to use the words of Father Richard Rohr. Father Rohr is a globally recognised ecumenical teacher and a Franciscan priest.

I particularly remember the Elisabeth Kubler-Ross "Life, Death, and Transition" workshop. At this experiential workshop, we were asked to complete a spontaneous drawing with crayons. I remember my drawing was of a ski field, and on the left hand side was the Poma lift. I needed to ride this lift in order to reach the top of the mountain. First, fear had to be conquered. I needed to stay calm, with my skis firmly planted, and with my eyes focussed on the top of the mountain, rather than seeing my wobbly skis and the deep valley on my left. There were green pine trees scattered in the drawing. These may have represented obstructions to avoid, but also the colour green reminds me of the heart chakra and growth in the plant kingdom as well as in my soul. My mentor at that workshop asked me, referring to the color white, what it was I was covering up? On reflection there were many struggles and hardships that needed to be blanketed from sight at that time or else the task of private palliative care nursing would have been too daunting. The old adage reminded me that we are not given more than we can bear. Most noteworthy in my drawing, however, was the figure of my skiing self, which clearly showed the skis pointing uphill rather than downhill!

While following my calling, I learned to work, and to give, and not to count the cost! "Give and don't count the cost" was the mantra that invaded my thoughts in those early years of pioneering work, and it remains with me to this day. Clearly, there were times when debts outweighed assets, and my private income was needed for survival. In the final years of secondary school I had studied accounting and, building on my work in my husband's orthodontic practice, I had a good understanding of business principles. Without a God-sensed commitment, colleagues left the company for more security, but this was not an option I considered. Someone comforted me by saying that a bright light attracts moths as well as butterflies. At the beginning of the Elisabeth Kubler-Ross workshop, we were asked to share our strengths and weaknesses with the group. I remember saying that my strength was that I was comfortable in the face of death. My weakness was that I was not good at failure. That could have been my ego talking, as egos are not good at failure or change. On reflection, the white snow did indeed cover up events that would refine my personality in a soul-making way.

Carolyn Myss, a contemporary mystic and teacher, writes that self-examination, prayer and contemplation are still the best ways to transfer ones centre of power from the external world to the interior world. She warns us to expect one obstacle after another and one trial after another. Looking back, I can see the truth in those words. Another author who shaped my world at that time was the religious psychiatrist M. Scott Peck. He wrote that each one of us must make our own path through life, as there are no self-help manuals, no formulas, and no easy answers. I can relate to his statement that life is a rocky path through the wilderness and also that, if this is accepted, difficulties no longer matter and a crisis can indeed become a challenge.

I take comfort in the Buddhist teaching that pain is what we measure pleasure by. I used to say that heaven could be boring if a constant state of bliss was experienced without a contrast. I felt there must be a bigger picture and believed, as had Florence Nightingale, that heaven was neither a place nor a time. My inquiring mind needed to learn and to understand the larger cosmic picture and the journey of the soul after death. Patients and mystics became my best teachers. There is wisdom to be found in connecting with those who are dying when one's personal ego takes a backseat, and there is a sense of being held in a sacred space rather than an approach that says: "How sad!" "How Terrible!" "He/she has lost the battle!"

These were my life-challenging questions:

- What am I called to do?
- Who am I called to become?
- What is the next step I need to take?
- Who can mentor me?
- What dragons do I need to face?
- What treasure do I need to find?
- What gifts do I need to bring to others?

While traveling to East and West Malaysia over a ten-year period, I was introduced to Eastern ways of honouring life and death, and to Islam. For a Muslim, the purpose of existence is to worship God and to obey God's will. For people with this belief, it is considered disrespectful to show personal grief at the time of death. Teaching grief and loss in Malaysia is very different to the Western experience.

A Western experience largely looks at grief from an individual's experience, and losses include the loss of possessions, homeland, personal status, and the death of loved ones. An Islamic approach is to understand grief alongside hope, when Allah has promised comfort and strength right into the valley of the shadow of death and beyond. I feel comfortable with an esoteric approach that views death as another step in the soul's journey, and appreciate that people view the soul, or Higher Self, through many different lenses.

In *Life Lessons: How Our Mortality can Teach Us about Life and Living* by Elisabeth Kubler-Ross and David Kessler, the Elisabeth Kubler-Ross Five Stages of Loss are defined in a way that illustrate the growth that loss has the power to initiate. The stages, which are neither linear nor applicable to all instances are: denial, anger, bargaining, depression, and acceptance. While they are helpful for deep understanding they can also be used as labels. This is not helpful. One lesson that I remember clearly from the

Life, Death, and Transition workshop was that emotions, healthy and unhealthy, represent a pocket of pus that needs to be released, so that healing can take place from the bottom up. Following a shamanic healing session with Cherie Sutherland, the author of *Transformed by the Light: Life After Near Death Experiences,* I learned that I had frequently buried my joy as well as negative emotions. From the contemporary spiritual teacher, Eckhart Tolle, I learned about the 'pain-body,' which is Tolle's term for the accumulation of old emotional pain that almost all people carry in their energy field. It is fed by negative thinking. Tolle writes:

> When thinking ceases to be clouded by emotion; your present perceptions are no longer distorted by the past. The energy that was trapped in the pain-body then changes its vibrational frequency and is transmuted into Presence.

Western ways of counselling and supporting a person in grief are not always appropriate in an Eastern culture. For example, I was accustomed to sending a card to the most significant person on the first Anniversary of my patient's death. Sending a card was not a custom familiar to East Malaysians. The Chinese community had specific in-depth rituals for the days and weeks following the death. I loved the story one Malay nurse told of how her family expressed their grief. As part of a ritual the family members placed a large leaf on their head and sank below the water of a nearby stream where the flowing water took the leaf away. The power of this ritual was to have a sense of the soul they loved leaving them.

On one of my visits to Sandakan Hospice, I was taken to visit a long house on the Sarawak River. Sarawak is a Malaysian state on the island of Borneo. Having been welcomed by the chief of the long house we were taken to the meeting room where a circle of human skulls was hanging from the roof. These skulls were receiving smoke from a fire burning beneath them in a ritual to appease their souls. In the practice of headhunting, the soul of the adversary was in this way being respected. Today, the powerful act of forgiveness takes a less brutal form in this culture, but the importance of ritual remains. For the Iban people of this region, life and health are dependent upon the condition of the soul. Death rituals, including chanting, are lengthy and complex.

Rituals touch aspects of our mind and heart. In my practice, the sending of an Anniversary card was a simple ritual. Other rituals are more complex and they include church services, marches, celebrations - personal and national - and special food for special occasions. Music in its many forms underpins many rituals. There may be fasting, feasting and gift giving. Rituals are attached to every milestone in life as well as death. The sharing of rituals for grief and for disposing of the, no longer needed, body is one way of forming understanding between religions and cultures as rituals go beyond words. End-of-life rituals include lighting the funeral pyre and lowering the coffin at the end of a funeral service, as well as rituals such as releasing birds, lighted lamps and balloons. In ancient Greece, there was a ritual of libation. This is when wine, or other liquid, is poured onto the earth as an offering to God in memory of those who have died. Pericles, the ancient Greek Statesman (495–427 BC), wisely said: "What you leave behind is not what is engraved on stone monuments, but what is woven into the lives of others."

My time spent in East Malaysia was enriched by listening to heart-felt sharing. I heard many stories of not being wanted or loved because of gender or some other circumstance of birth. In any culture, it seems that early childhood wounds have long-lasting effects and influence the person's lifetime for good or ill. I use a personal example. As a middle-aged adult, I gained insight into my strained relationship with my father. As a small child, my favorite pet was a mummy tabby cat who, from time to time, had kittens. Many of the kittens my father would drown as soon as they were born. I would follow mummy cat around and try to console her as she searched and meowed for her kittens. I saw the milk dripping from her teats and felt my cat's pain. Of course, it was explained to me by my parents that they could not keep all the kittens, and that they were trying to be kind by drowning them before their eyes were open. That explanation did not remove the pain.

On reflection, I see that my feelings and sensitivity for people who are dying, and those who are grieving, may have grown from such early childhood imprints. Stories such as mine are common, although the wounds vary. Child abuse comes in many forms and may well be the result of good intentions gone awry or simply due to ignorance, rather than a deliberate wish to cause harm.

I had many teachers in my early palliative care practice. Catholic nuns introduced me to the Myers-Briggs Typology Indicator (MBTI) and the work of Swiss psychologist C. G. Jung. Not only did I begin to know my own strengths and weaknesses, but I also learned to understand and appreciate differences between other people. Katherine Briggs and her daughter Isabel Briggs-Myer gave to the world the MBTI, which was an expansion of Jung's work. Their aim was to help people to see that by understanding differences in personality there would be more harmony in life. For me, it demonstrated that there is beauty to be found in difference, like in the orchestra, where different instruments play individual sounds to create one beautiful and harmonious piece of music. One of my students said that having knowledge of the Myers-Briggs typology saved her marriage. She realised that she was married to an introverted thinker while she was an extraverted feeler. Once understood, these differences became gifts.

The MBTI was my first adventure into knowing myself. "Know thyself" were the words on the famous temple at Delphi in ancient Greece. Not only did this tool assist me in knowing myself, it was most helpful in selecting and mentoring members of my caring team, because they could relate to these simply explained personality differences. Jung believed that each human being has a specific nature and calling which is uniquely his or her own. With this understanding, the journey of life has a meaning, and becomes more exciting and interesting. For me, it gave me my first insight into my intuitive, extroverted, feeling, and decisive personality, and to shovel away some of the "snow" I referred to earlier. On a professional level, I learned that if I was building rapport with a thinking person I needed to stick to the facts rather than ask about feelings, and that if I was to break bad news to an introvert, I needed to give them time to absorb the information before following up. It is the extravert who needs to talk, to put things outside in order to understand the news. It is the person with a preference for thinking that takes a long view of a situation and it is the person with a preference for feeling who takes a more personal view.

For many years, I used the MBTI program to assist participants in my education programs to gain insight into their personality. Eventually,

I took the qualifying course. During that training, I learned that to find one's spiritual path one needed to look at one's least preferred functions and strive to bring all the scores obtained by answering the questions into balance. This meant spending time looking at my introverted thinking as a function, rather than being comfortable with extroverted feeling. To become an introverted thinker, I needed to find time for deep reflection and for writing. This led me into the domain of meditation and to welcome silence. As an extroverted feeling personality, my preference was to receive energy from the outside world and to talk things over with other people in order to make sense of them. When my work was taken over by others in 2015, I was forced to work alone and to put this theory to the test. Meditation, lucid dreaming, and exploring past lives became priorities. My inborn temperament of being an intuitive feeler, at best, assists me to become my authentic self. Valuable spiritual experiences come from being in nature, meditation, listening to podcasts from contemporary mystics, and reading.

CHAPTER 4

Death and Beyond

Over nearly three decades of nursing people at the time of death it has been impossible for me not to question what comes next. Removing fear at the time of death has been a priority, but to do that I have shared that I believe there is life, in some form, after death. Indeed, one elderly man, who had been a mechanic, replied in a hoarse voice to this statement with, "There better be!" Common fears include:

- The process of dying. "I'm not afraid of dying but of how I might die."
- The unknown and going there alone. Dr. Derek Doyle, a palliative care doctor from Scotland, describes this experience as buying a platform ticket - the platform ticket takes one to the platform where the train departs, but only the dying person can board the train.
- Being unable to have wishes respected. A person may have a wish for assisted dying when they feel it is their time and be unable to do so because of unmet criteria and/or a doctor's opinion. They may have a wish to die in a chosen environment, town or country. Quality-of-life factors need to be considered—these are personal and individual.
- Not being accepted for oneself. "If I get angry or smelly, I won't be liked and no one will come to see to my needs..." Dr. Elisabeth Kubler-Ross, the Swiss Psychiatrist who taught the world so much

about death and dying, calls this the need for unconditional love, which is a universal need.

- Being unprepared or secure in a life philosophy. "I don't know if there is life after death," "I'm not sure I can face a loving God. I feel so guilty about so many things." This highlights the need for forgiveness of self and others. Forgiveness for the times when harsh words were said in reactive haste without a pause for a more appropriate response.
- Disappointing doctors and those who care. "If I don't take the treatment, they'll think I'm not trying, yet I want to be in charge of my living and dying."
- Not being listened to, understood, or receiving empathy. "I said that I had pain, but they told me that I couldn't have, as I had been given medication for pain." "I told them that I was OK but really I wanted someone to stay with me."
- Abandonment. "I wanted to use the bed pan and no one came." "The nights are so long and scary."
- Being helpless and dependent. "I can't even lift my head when my neck gets stiff or turn over when my body aches from being too long in one position."
- Time running out. "I haven't written to my brother to tell him I'm sorry for not giving him the help he needed." "I haven't said who can have my collection of fine porcelain."
- Causing sadness and hardship. "I know that my wife will miss me, as we have done everything together. I don't know how she will manage the garden by herself."
- Being incontinent. "I would feel terrible if I wet the bed and couldn't control my bowels and bladder."
- Looking awful. "I've always had my hair done." "I don't want people to see me with these yellow eyes." "I hate being seen without my dentures, yet my mouth is so sore."
- Fear of suffering. "I don't want my dying prolonged." "I want my Advance Care Directive followed."
- Not being given all the facts. "I wish they would tell me the results of the tests and what it all means."

- Being a burden. "My wife looks so tired when she comes to visit." "I feel I am needlessly spending my children's inheritance."
- Not making a future special event. "I just want to see my grandson married."
- Fear of not having enough reflective time. "People want to cheer me up and make me respond when all I want is to be quiet and feel in touch with my God." "I just want stillness rather than all this busy activity."
- Not being able to communicate my needs. "My thoughts turn to my children and grandchildren, but I'm too weak to speak and I want to give them my blessing." "If only someone would see my frowns and know that I was in pain." "The call bell is out of reach."
- Economic matters. "My care is costing a lot." "I haven't told my children about the life insurance policy or where to find the property deeds."
- Losing trusting relationships. "My doctor said that he would make sure that I did not have my death prolonged, but what if he is away and the new doctor doesn't know my wishes?"
- Not dying well. "I want to be an inspiration to my children." "I don't want the closing down of my body to be messy and smelly."
- Losing myself. "Mostly I feel confident and good about my life, but there are times when I feel frightened and insecure." "I had a frightening dream of losing my footing as I climbed a mountain."
- Fear of those around me being morbid and unaccepting of my desire to see death as my graduation from earth school. "I want to die in an atmosphere of love and laughter."

When I first began my career as a private palliative care nurse in 1987, I was asked to care for an elderly woman suffering from cancer. She told me, when I first met her in the unit which had become her home, that she was pleased that she had a terminal illness, although it upset her family. I did not ask why she felt this way. It seemed to be an unnecessary question, because there was such an atmosphere of peace and acceptance in the room, and I was respectful of her decision to welcome death. This woman had given her life to the selfless tasks of translating books into braille and to raising another woman's children as her own. I stayed with her for several nights until another referral called me away. When I told her that the coming night was to be my last with her, she said, "It's alright, Joy, we have met many times before and we will meet again." I replied that Elisabeth Kubler-Ross said that the wisest people on earth are those who are dying and know it. In a calm and steady voice, her comment was: "I think she may be right."

From that time, I have been searching to make sense of the big questions in life. My journeying has taken me to seek wisdom in Eastern Philosophy, Sufi Mysticism and Energy modalities such as Reiki and Therapeutic Touch. On visiting the USA for Therapeutic Touch conferences, I met the founders Delores Krieger, PhD, RN, Professor Emeritus of Nursing at New York University, and Dora Kunz, a gifted energy healer. For many years, I was a member of the Nurse Healers' Association in the United States of America and attended their conferences. I was introduced to the healing practices of the Native American Indians and 'in general' began to appreciation the connectedness of the mind, body and spirit or soul, and the healing powers of energy. One of my carers said to me one day in a debriefing session; "Joy, you can't kill a soul." I believe this to be true, and I ponder on the question as to why death is still such a fearsome and taboo subject. In *The Tibetan Book of Living and Dying*, Sogyal Rinpoche quotes Dr. Elisabeth Kubler-Ross: "When people come to grips with their own dying, then we would respect patients' needs and listen to them, and would not have a problem such as fear of dying."

Palliative care is care that extends to family and loved ones and seeks to combine the latest technology with compassion and understanding. It acknowledges that the love of family and friends is important medicine, and that support beginning at diagnosis will maximise the quality of the end-of-life process. Stephen Levine, the author of the book *Who Dies?*, writes that when fears are removed there is no need for hope, because a state of peace will exist where the person is living fully in the moment. His book parts the veil between this world and the next for the reader and encourages all to participate fully in life as the perfect preparation for whatever may come next. Death need not be a fearsome monster to be avoided at all costs and an event that requires mountains of legalisation and protection against. Life is an energy current that gets turned on at birth and turned off at death.

In my early nurse practice, I spoke to many people who'd experienced near-death experiences and communications from the unseen world. One woman told of her experience during an asthma episode. She said that she was floating near the ceiling of the bedroom and saw her dressing gown behind the door, as well as her own body on the bed. It is not uncommon for a person who is near death to see forms that bring comfort. One daughter reported that her mother was looking at a blank wall and smiling and nodding as if she was seeing a vision she recognised. Another woman told me that she experienced receiving a message from another reality following the death by accident of her eighteen-year-old son. It had been a shattering loss until she saw her son's dog swimming lengths of her swimming pool. The dog hated water and wouldn't go near the pool normally, and yet here it was giving this mother a sign that her son was fine and doing laps in another dimension.

Florence Nightingale wrote in *Suggestions for Thought* that she believed our life purpose is to come from imperfection to perfection and that we needed more than one lifetime to do so. Reincarnation was a common belief in her lifetime (1820–1910). For example, Max Muller (1823–1900), a founder of Comparative Religious studies who lived and studied in Great Britain for most of his life, introduced concepts of reincarnation by means of his translations of Indian scriptures. He wrote:

> I cannot help thinking that the souls towards whom we feel drawn in this life are the very souls whom we knew and loved in the former life, and the souls who repel us here but we do not know why, are souls that earned our disapproval, the souls from whom we kept aloof in a former life.

Nightingale's private education included Ancient Greek, Latin, French, German, Italian, history, philosophy, and mathematics. She translated Plato, her favourite philosopher, in her teens and was introduced to Jewish, Christian, Islamic, and Hindu scriptures, as well as the Persian mystic Rumi. She prized freedom of thought, and saw it as a privilege for oneself and a quality to respect in others. I feel in agreement with her writings and also appreciate the wisdom to be found in all religions. I smile to myself on her views on marriage, as it was 'in' the Victorian era. She wrote that a married woman did not exist in the eyes of the law (no money in her own name nor voting rights or education) and if she was to follow her own interests, these had to be at odd moments.

Rumi's poetry speaks to me.

> When I die
> when my coffin
> is being taken out
> you must never think
> I am missing this world
>
> don't shed any tears
> don't lament or
> feel sorry
> I'm not falling
> into a monster's abyss
>
> when you see
> my corpse is being carried
> don't cry for my leaving
> I'm not leaving
> I'm arriving at eternal love…

An important concern for me is how to support an aging population to gracefully transition from this world to the next with an attitude of faith rather than fear. I feel sad when I walk through a nursing home and see so many men and women just waiting for their bodies and minds to break down completely before releasing their souls. An opposite feeling came to mind when I heard a grandson say about his grandfather's death: "My grandfather didn't fall off his perch, he stepped off!" At my early Elisabeth Kubler Ross workshop, I learned that I can only take people along the final path successfully to the extent that I have tried to make sense of the path myself. Nursing is so much more than clinical observation, hygiene, and nutrition. Many resources are spent on obligatory reporting and imposing regulations that seem to dampen spirits, at the expense of personal spontaneity and expressions of love and laughter.

In *New Nursing*, I gave simple suggestions for caring to be more focused on the whole person. I have a belief in quality people in charge and mentoring, rather than quality assurance measures that impose actions and data collection instead of promoting a loving natural flow of energy. Respect and kindness in a peace filled environment have the potential to transform parts of a person's character which are not as healthy as they could be. Like Florence Nightingale, the founder of modern nursing, I feel nursing is a vocation. She believed that education and work provided the proper circumstances for the Divine Will to come forth. A change of attitude and the intention to promote excellence in end-of-life care are needed to actively prepare people for their final breath.

This approach is different to one that focuses on physical care, entertainment, and longevity - in some cases without quality of life. The most important care people need at the end of their life is to have their soul needs met. They need to be guided through a process of completion. When energy leaves the body, it has completed its cycle and carries its karma into the next realm of awareness. People need instructions and conversations on how to best complete this phase, if that is their choice. Soul needs are primary to excellence in aged care.

I have had many teachers in almost three decades of caring, and most insights seemed to have been gained at the bedside rather than from books. Jack Kornfield, the author and teacher of Buddhist Psychology, gives this description of the difference between love and attachment:

> Attachment masquerades as love. It says, "I will love this person because I need them." Or, "I'll love you if you'll love me back. I'll love you, but only if you will be the way I want." This isn't love at all – it is attachment – and unhealthy attachment is rigid; it is very different from love. When there is attachment, there is clinging and fear. Love allows, honors, and appreciates; attachment grasps, demands, needs, and aims to possess.

Joseph Campbell, the great mythologist, wrote that we all need to tell our story and to understand our story. He believed that for life to signify it needed to touch the eternal in significant ways. Listening to personal stories is a big part of healing as a person faces the last phase of life. Sogyal Rinpoche, the author of the *Tibetan Book of Living and Dying,* writes that the Tibetan Buddhist masters tell us that we should die peacefully. He further states that sometimes people hold onto life and are afraid to let go and die, because they have not come to terms with what they have been and done in this lifetime. Other writers on death preparation have also used the phrase "unfinished business" and recommend ways to bring about its resolution. It is heartening to see biographies being facilitated in the hospice setting. It would be great to see this practice extended to aged care facilities.

In my understanding, a good death is not a quick fix from physical, emotional, nor spiritual suffering. It's in knowing that it is time. What is needed is for all concerned to be comfortable with conversations about death and dying. Death needs to be made visible. I remember being present for the death of an elderly woman in an aged care facility. Other residents would often come into the room and know that something was not right, although they were suffering from dementia. I would talk to them and say something positive about the person who was dying. Yet it was the policy of that aged care facility to shut residents in their rooms while the person who had died was being transferred to the funeral home, and not talk about the event. I thought at the time that there needed to be a guard of honour made up of residents and a path strewn with flowers. In other words, a meaningful ritual that was death-affirming needed to be part of the policy. One facility I visited had a chapel for residents, and on arriving for a funeral to be held there, I found rows of walkers lined up like cars! Other residents were not only involved but reassured that their turn would be special.

Communication, on the conscious and the unconscious level, is the key to unblocking unfinished business. Because symbols can be more powerful than words, the simple activity of pasting cut-out pictures and photos onto a sheet of cardboard in a reflective mood can facilitate a peeling back of the layers of memory to give insight. I call this "soul collage," when it is done meditatively. Other names like "vision boards" or "memory boards" are given.

> *When the soul wishes to experience something, she throws an image of the experience out before her, and enters into her own image.*
>
> —Meister Eckart

In a state of stillness, a picture or image may bring new understanding to a past event or situation. One of my patients became aware that she needed to be more independent and to claim her abilities just by reflecting on the image of a car. When her husband was alive, he made it his duty to fill her car with fuel. Now that he had died, she was more appreciative of this small act. Images are reminders of a soul's journey, and thoughts and feelings once brought to light can be managed and healed. In this way, a significant event can be recalled at a deeper level of awareness while contemplating a simple picture of a small flower, caged bird, or towering mountain.

Time allotted just for listening is rare in our busy world. When possible, I tried to combine listening with daily activities such as bed making, drying a back or massaging legs. One elderly woman who was nursed in her own home would frequently call me to patch up a skin tear on her legs. As I applied the heavy ulcer dressing to hold the skin tear in place, I would gently massage her legs and give a little loving-touch pressure over the dressing. At these times, she would talk about her life - it wasn't eyeball to eyeball as my gaze was directed at the wound. Hairdressers report that they experience the same intimate conversations. I joked with her one day and said that I thought she banged her shin on purpose just so I would have to visit. How good would it have been if I had made a nurse visit without a particular reason? While I was at boarding school, someone wrote in my autograph book: "The greatest things we do in life we do unknowingly."

This was the case for Ken, who was in his nineties and very deaf. He and his wife, who was blind, lived in their own home, and my assistants would give them total care. Among other complaints Ken had gangrenous toes, which he refused to have amputated. As the gangrene spread so the pain relieving medications were increased. His bed was put in the living room so that he could watch cricket and he enjoyed the summer of cricket before he died. One day, when I had returned from a holiday in Broome, Western Australia, I told Ken about the tiny little birds on the mud flats there. There were hundreds of them, and each year I was told they migrated to China. I thought this was an opportunity to ask Ken if he could feel like one of those birds and toss his body into the air for the currents of wind to take him home. There was a pause, and then he replied: "Joy, you would be more use if you scratched my back!" Some things do not need to be said, intention seems enough. After Ken died, I was tidying the room and came across his diary. I flicked though the mostly empty pages and was surprised to see the words, sometimes months apart and in a shaky hand: "Joy came."

Like Ken, all people are allowed to refuse medical treatment. Yet in the aged care sector concerns about body weight and being sat out of bed seem to be a priority over resolving "unfinished business" and sharing fears and questions about what comes after death. The principal of informed consent requires that all options are given to the patient. Yet death or letting nature take its course, is seldom included. It seems to be much easier to offer a pacemaker for the heart than to lift the weight of unresolved grief and to unburden a soul. Emotional and spiritual needs are many and individual.

It is not the body and physical needs that need to take priority at the end of someone's life. It is rather setting the mind to make some sense of the ups and downs, good times and bad times and lessons learned along the way, that bring peace and insight. Being reminded of experiences of love and holding that feeling in one's heart–mind while breathing deeply is what I encouraged for the soul's departure. This can complement the medications that may be required to make the body that comfortable place to live in while the soul makes preparation for departure. In my experience, the giving of medications need not be feared. The soul seems to know when it is time to leave. This leaving seems to be unrelated to the doses of medication that may be given in a hospice setting.

One of my early patients taught me the satisfaction of living a full life. I had been asked by the hospice to visit a man in his sixties who had cancer, and to tell him about what the hospice offered. Andrew's wife led me to where he was sitting in a high-backed chair in his den, and introduced me. He was jaundiced and his stomach was very swollen, yet his face beamed, and he said, "Joy, I might only be sixty but I lived eighty years. I've played A grade cricket and A grade golf and I was successful and happy with my business and family. I don't need a hospice as I'm happy to spend my days at home." I don't know what gave this man his inner strength, but I could sense that he was comfortably in control. As I grew more confident with asking the God question I received many and varied answers from: "I think God is your conscience"; "I think God is like the ocean and I am a grain of sand"; "I feel closest to God when I watch a sunset." Invariably, I would pay close attention to my intuition for guidance on what to say and when to be silent. Dying is a sacred act and needs respect and support.

I believe that we are energy beings or forms, filled with light energy. Eckhart Tolle writes in his book *A New Earth* that energy is the bridge between form and formless. It is a scientific fact that energy cannot be destroyed. The question arises of what happens to a person's energy when death occurs or the link between form and formless is broken? For many family members and health professionals who are present at the time of death there is a profound sense of lifelessness. "They are gone!" I like to think that the energy or life force has left the body and carries the "DNA" of the soul with it into the other side of the veil which separates this world and the next. Maybe in that space, some "genetic modification" takes place before the rebirth.

In Buddhist teaching, mind is not part of the body which dies, along with ego, at the time of death. Mind - or soul - lives on. I remember inviting an elderly woman who was near death to think of something she had done well in her life and to hold the feeling in her mind. There was no need to share what had been recalled in her imagination, and I suggested that it may be to arrange a bowl of flowers, bake a cake, or raise a child. When she indicated that she had an event I invited her to be a lump of butter on a hot piece of toast. She said: "And just melt away." She died several days later.

DNA is a molecule that carries most of the genetic instructions used in the development, functioning and reproduction of all known living organisms and many viruses. I like to think that there is such a molecule that carries the state of the soul into its next lifetime. Hindu wisdom traditions have in common the notion of karma and reincarnation. Obviously, our tiny minds, too often led by ego, find it difficult to comprehend such profound teachings. A Hindu guide on a holiday to Bali explained to me that the Balinese people know there is one great God but their minds find it difficult to relate to the One Greatness.

As a way of connecting with an influence greater than their daily life, they pay homage to small gods such as Dewi Sri, the goddess of rice. In the grounds of my small hotel in Ubud, it was common to see small woven reed trays filled with flowers placed in the garden as an offering to the gods. The Hindu Balinese have many rituals, including rituals for after death. These gentle Hindu people are an inspiration to me when I compare that gentleness with the atmosphere of a busy modern hospital.

All those involved in health care can appreciate the subtle force of Love and be aware when Love is in action. The Biblical saying that "God is love" is something that my mind can imagine. Holding on to a feeling of love, by whatever image, is a powerful tool for facilitating a good night's sleep, as well as preparing for the eternal sleep. For some, the "love trigger" is nature and for others it might be a Holy image or a connectedness between two people. I like to imagine the result of all doctors and nurses being loving presences! Instead, the emphasis is on making sure the documentation has legal rather than loving priorities.

A simple ritual like lighting a candle can be powerful. I recall an elderly Catholic woman, who was very fearful of dying. She sat in her chair day and night. It seemed that a part of her psyche was saying, "If you lie down you will die." I said to her that one day I might find her dead in her chair. Her reply was, "Well, I won't worry will I?" I said that if that was her attitude then I wouldn't worry either. Patient-centred care means finding ways to honour those little rituals and behaviors. A neighbour came in once when Agnes was, in fact, in bed and dying. This neighbour was a Catholic nun and she felt that she would like to give Agnes the candle she received when she took her vows. The candle burned for days, and when it was finally extinguished Agnes also took her last breath. Another memory is of a family who filled the room where their dying mother lay with lighted candles. The explanation was that they were lighting the way for her.

When a person is near death many observe a special glow about them. This may be understood as the form of condensed energy which carried the soul reducing its energy and density to allow the Eternal Light to shine through. This is a time when near-death experiences occur. The person who is dying may report that they are seeing people who have already died. I remember the room of a person near death that became very warm, although the window was open and the other rooms in the house were cold. Death and the process of dying is the doorway to the mystery of life, and yet it is rarely talked about. All people facing the end of their life need to have the opportunity to discuss in positive terms what is in front of them. It is up to nurses and health professionals to educate and support people when their journey on earth is coming to an end.

Care that does not encompass the soul's needs is inadequate. In a caring role there is an exchange of energy between two people. When the energy of the carer is unhealthy, care at the bedside is diminished. Death is a doorway to what comes next and needs to go beyond traditional medical care. The term 'holistic care' is being used more commonly to refer to comprehensive care that integrates physical, intellectual, emotional, and spiritual needs. Spiritual needs are often referred to as aesthetic needs, as they cannot be seen with the physical eye or, indeed, measured with observations. They include beauty in some form: a painting, a verse, or the sound of music. It is difficult to change attitudes to end-of-life care when the health system is set up to promote what can be measured and seen. Soul needs are everyone's responsibility, as we all need to find meaning and purpose. The more soulful a caring facility is, the more love and compassion thrives.

In 2014, I travelled with Jean Houston to Greece to explore the Golden Age of Greece. Jean is a world-renowned scholar, philosopher, and leader in human capacities. I have spent many years listening to her work. One of the lessons I learned in Greece was about the "Myth of Er." This myth is a legend that concludes Plato's *Republic*. The story includes an account of the cosmos and the afterlife that greatly influenced religious, philosophical, and scientific thought for many centuries. Socrates tells Glaucon the "Myth of Er" to explain that the choices we make and the character we develop will have consequences after death. When Er, who was a Greek warrior, dies in battle and revives on his funeral pyre, he tells of his journey into the afterlife. Today, we would call it a near-death experience. The tale introduces the idea that moral people are rewarded and immoral people punished after death, and that the soul is immortal. Socrates died in 399 BCE, and yet this belief lives on with many interpretations. These ideas are fertile ground for exploring the purpose of life and for considering the soul's journey through many lifetimes.

Today, writers like Jean Houston teach the benefits of reflecting on a life, and having the opportunity to change one's perception of events which have provided invisible wounding. In the women's groups that I have enjoyed, so many women proudly said that they went on to be successful business or professional women in their own right following a traumatic event in their lives. It was so for me when my marriage ended after a period of thirty years. I have been without a partner for more than two decades, and while I value the experience of being responsible for my life and being able to live alone, my connection to the unseen world is a constant companion. Lessons of compassion, forgiveness and understanding are many. My four children, and now twelve grandchildren, were gifts, and a part of my destiny.

In my role of counsellor, I would not give advice, but rather empower people to find their own insights and solutions. This practice involves looking at a problem or life experience from different angles. A strategy I would often use was to ask a person about the best and worst times of their life. For example, one independent woman responded to this question with an answer that told of her business successes and also of being adopted as a baby. Now facing a debilitating and slow death, she was intent on crawling to the bathroom, although she could walk with a frame. My intuition told me that this woman was craving a tender mother's love rather than the tough love approach and minimum impersonal care suggested by her brother, who stood to gain from her death. Yes, there were many contributing factors, but when I gave her a hug and held her, she softened into the hug as if craving the love of an absent mother.

Returning to the Myth of Er; with other souls, Er had come across an awe-inspiring place with four openings, two into and out of the sky and two into and out of the earth or underworld. Judges sat between the openings, but Er was instructed to listen and observe and report his experience to mankind. After some time, Er and the souls came to the Spindle of Necessity and, in order, were asked to choose their next life. The spindle represented a map of the cosmos and its planets. Many, having experienced the upper and lower world, choose a life different to their previous experience. Some chose wisely, but others made choices while being ignorant of the consequences of their choices. It may have been a choice to live a royal life or to be a famous actor or actress, without realising the lack of a private life or the steps needed to be taken in order to achieve the goal. In this myth, it is suggested that philosophy will break the cycle of reward and punishment.

In his book *Life after Death*, Deepak Chopra writes that with the possibility of infinite lifetimes extending forward and backward, a soul could experience hundreds of heavens and hells. His message is that death is not the end and, during life, the physical body provides a garment for the soul. He writes that there is abundant evidence that "the world beyond" is not separated from this world by an impassable wall; in fact, a single reality embraces all worlds, all times and places, and at the end of our lives we cross over into a new phase of the same soul journey. Lionel Fifield from the Relaxation Centre in Brisbane gives the analogy of many people being on a stage while a spotlight may only illumine one person. Just because the others cannot be seen doesn't mean that they do not exist.

Carolyn Myss writes in *Sacred Contracts* about the lessons a person chooses to learn in a lifetime and the guidance given to that individual. Pierre Teilhard de Chardin wrote, "We are not human beings having a spiritual experience. We are spiritual beings having a human experience." In Plato's myth, the souls travelled to the Plane of Oblivion and the River of Forgetfulness (Lethe) when they drank some of the water before their rebirth.

Socrates wrote: "The unexamined life is not worth living." To assist a person who is about to part the veil between this world and the next, recalling the highs and lows of experiences can give some meaning to an event, and perhaps the event can be viewed in a different and more positive light. Sogyal Rinpoche, the Tibetan Buddhist master, says that death is the mirror in which we review life. The following wisdom is from Florence Nightingale:

> As each individual embodies unique qualities that cannot be duplicated, it would not be consistent with God's benevolent nature to obliterate that being. Because it is God's plan to raise mankind from imperfection to perfection, death must initiate a different mode of existence, one that allows for continued development.

CHAPTER 5

Religion and Spirituality

On an initial visit to an elderly gentleman, I asked if he belonged to a religion. The reply from this smiling and seemingly at peace man was that he had visits from the Anglican priest, and sometimes went to mass in the Catholic Church but thought he would be buried under his mother's banner, which was the Uniting Church. Many have replied to that question by saying that they are such and such, but that it is only a label. I learned in establishing my patients' spiritual supports to ask if the religion given was indeed a source of comfort or just a label. I would at times actively encourage the patient and family to have a visit from a priest or minister of their religion - perhaps saying that it is not a bad idea to have a bet both ways. This meant that you can die in your own way with your own thoughts on the topic of what happens after death, or perhaps a prayer or two could be helpful in preparing the soul to leave the body. I remember one patient who lived by the sea. When I asked about his faith or religion he answered, "I can see a daffodil from my window and the sea behind it, and that is enough for me." A decline in traditional religious observance is evident in many parts of the world. Yet there is a need for food that nourishes the soul, perhaps in a new form that facilitates a direct personal line with the sacred?

In the face of death, people do change their thinking on all things spiritual, and I like to validate a change, but feel that this needs to be done with great sensitivity. The danger is for the health professional to suggest what has been helpful to him or her on their particular soul journey. Each person is an individual soul with his or her own soul destiny. When I was working in Malaysia next to an old folk's home, there would be a visit from a Christian minister every Friday, and there would be great jubilation if a resident of the home 'is' converted to Christianity. This made me very uncomfortable. When I visited the Ashram of Saccidanama in Southern India in 2015 with Andrew Harvey, I was impressed with the teachings of John Martin Sahajananda who succinctly combines Indian-Christian Spirituality with Hinduism. At the Ashram, I was given a booklet titled *O Lord Make Us Instruments of Your Peace: Mission without Conversion.* This said much!

John Martin Sahajananda, who continues to teach in the Ashram where Bede Griffith, the great master of Christian spiritual consciousness taught, writes in his book *The Four O'clock Talks*:

> The role of any religion needs to be to help people to purify their egos. Converting people from one religion to another is like taking people from one branch of the tree, or from one ego, to another. Is it right to take people from one branch to another, or is it better that we help people to move beyond the branches? Christ was not focused on converting people from one religion to another, but rather on opening the door to go beyond the religions.

Before I can purify my ego, I need to understand how ego impacts my life. In his book *A New Earth,* Eckhart Tolle gives many insights into ego.

> It consists of thought and emotion, of a bundle of memories you identify with as "me and my story," of habitual roles you play without knowing it, of collective identifications such as nationality, religion, race, social class, or political allegiance. It also contains personal identifications, not only with possessions, but also with opinions, external appearance, long-standing resentments, or concepts of yourself as better than or not as good as others, as a success or failure.

Just how can one achieve giving unconditional love, compassion and service to others without being ego driven? For Sufi mystics, Karen Armstrong, in her book *A History of God,* writes that the systematic destruction of the ego led to a sense of absorption in a larger, ineffable reality, and this was a Sufi ideal for greater self-realism, self-control and a return to the Source of his being. God was discovered to be mysteriously identified with the inmost self. This inmost self was the self that he was meant to be. A Rumi quote from the Web: "Kill the cow of your ego as quickly as you can, so that your inner spirit can come to light, and attain true awareness." This line of thinking is about spirituality rather than religion, and I find that many people relate to general themes of spirituality. Father Richard Rohr in his meditation on Universal Wisdom introduced me to The Perennial Tradition. In this religious philosophy, the view is held that esoteric and exoteric themes stem from the same source. These consistently recurring themes say:

- There is a Divine Reality underneath and inherent in the world of things;
- There is in the human soul a natural capacity, similarity, and longing for this Divine Reality;
- The final goal of existence is union with this Divine Reality.

One day, while taking a taxi to the airport, my driver inquired about my journey. I told him that I was joining a pilgrimage to Medjugorje with Caroline Myss, whose teachings have been guiding me for more than twenty years. My driver was a young man who was casually dressed and not a typical student driver earning his university fees. He told me that he was interested in deeper truths and had been attending some lectures. He had identified with the Divine Reality that runs through all after gazing at the beauty of a sunset and the wonder of a baby's birth. He said that these events have the power to affect everyone on the Earth regardless of race or creed.

In the terminal phase of a person's life the conversations around the bed often include seeing a loved one who has already died or receiving a message from someone who has already died. These conversations are not rational in the everyday world, but do not seem out of place in the face of death. My goal was to be an open, calm and non-judgemental loving presence, and to mentally invite peaceful energy to come through me. This energy exchange with a person in the terminal phase of life is difficult to achieve in a health care setting where people come and go and are busy with medical tasks.

Bede Griffiths' book, *The Marriage of East and West,* was given to me in 1994 by the nurse in charge of St. Leonard's Hospice in York, England. A visit to this site was part of an International Hospice and Palliative Care Study Seminar in the UK. I was amazed at the wisdom that book contained. Bede Griffiths, who was a British-born Benedictine monk and priest, wrote that there is a craving for warmth, for closeness, and for intimacy in every human being. In my practice, I would encourage my assistants to give their love to patients. There have been times when holding a patient has been the only form of comfort that could be given when there was no medication available.

This brings memories of a man who had chosen to stay at home with his faithful dog by his side for the last period of his life. He was settled for the night, sitting upright and supported by many pillows in his double bed. I sat myself on the bed and leant on the side of his pillows where I could stroke his arm. In the early hours of the morning, he woke up and leaned forward. I fanned his back with his pyjama coat as he was hot and sweaty, and asked if he had any pain. He replied with a twinkle in his eye as he observed me on the bed: "Not now!" I replied: "It is a pity you can't tell your mates at the university where you worked that you had a blonde nurse in bed with you all night!" It was a precious love-sharing exchange. He died several days later. I remember standing with some of his carers at the foot of his bed and offering a toast to his life.

Another patient was to open my eyes to the wisdom of religious psychiatrist, M. Scott Peck. On reading his book *A Different Drum*, I could relate to the four stages of spirituality which he described. The first stage is the chaos of angry manipulative people (acting like wilful children or only doing a good deed if there is something in it for them). The second stage is when these people commit themselves to an institution like the church or the army, where there are rules and regulations to keep them on the straight and narrow path. The third stage is when these people begin to question these rules and norms and begin to look for good (God) outside the religious or other institutions. The fourth stage is when people discover a direct line with the Divine within. This is most often through mindfulness and meditation. When I asked my patient about her religion she replied that she used to be a regular churchgoer and even played the organ for church services, but that now she no longer attended church. I told her that she was lucky as she only had one more stage to go before she had her direct line to God, according to M. Scott Peck, MD. She smiled knowingly.

Conversations concerning religion and spiritual beliefs are necessary for excellence in end-of-life care. Death is after all about the soul leaving the physical body. Having established the views, experiences and beliefs of people, an appropriate language can be chosen. I value the insights I have gained from Buddhism, and if it is appropriate I may offer a Buddhist quote such as: "Pain and suffering come with attachment and aversion." This opens the door to things and people who may be keeping the person who is facing death from reaching that final stage of peace and acceptance, as described by Dr. Elisabeth Kubler-Ross. Her books are many, and I like the way she describes death as the final stage of growth.

Attachments to memories are painful when emotions such as hatred, jealousy, envy, arrogance, dishonesty and vengeance are given holding space in our psyche. A metaphor for peace may be the image of a tranquil lake, which is not disturbed by wind, animal, or human action. The value of imagination and the use of visualisation cannot be underestimated for changing a situation to one that is desired from one that is causing distress. A person may be encouraged to breathe in love and to breathe out the emotion that is eroding their peace-filled heart. Forgiveness may be visualised by seeing the people involved giving each other flowers and a hug, while a release may involve cutting imaginary threads which are connected to the situation.

For ten years from 1998, I travelled annually to Sandakan in East Malaysia for the purpose of training hospice volunteers, and supporting the work of their community based hospice. In my time in West Malaysia in 1996, I learned much about Eastern philosophies. I learned that pain was often viewed as an essential part of karma and, as such, relief provided from medications was not requested or accepted. It seemed that suffering in this world could help in the choice of a more favourable rebirth in the next. When I worked in the Mary Potter Hospice in Adelaide, I met a man who did not want his pain removed because it reminded him of the pain associated with feelings of love. This seemed an extreme description of a holistic perspective. Yet I know from the teachings of Jean Houston that feelings and memories of love and pleasure can be mentally placed in areas of pain to give relief. I am reminded of the writings of my good friend Geri Marr Burdman, who is a gerontologist in the United States. As a student of Dr. Viktor Frankl, she emphasises the value of finding meaning in suffering. In his book *Man's Search for Meaning*, Frankl writes, "When we are no longer able to change a situation, we are challenged to change ourselves."

The bestselling author, Tony Buzan, in his book, *The Power of Spiritual Intelligence* writes, "When a person is Spiritually Intelligent you become aware of the big picture, for self and the universe and your place and purpose in it." He credits Florence Nightingale with being a great spiritually intelligent individual, as I do. Florence Nightingale questioned all religions, and her questionings are recorded by Janet Macrae and Michael D. Calabria in their editing of her writings: *Suggestions for Thought by Florence Nightingale, Selections and Commentaries* published in 1994. Also, Val Webb wrote a valuable book, *Florence Nightingale: The Making of a Radical Theologian*. I associated with Nightingale's ideas on mysticism and the need to go within, as well as her belief that men and women have souls to unfold and have a part to play in God's great world.

On reflecting on God's great world, I had an image which has stayed with me ever since a trip to Tibet. Feeling too tired to climb the many hundred steps to the Buddhist temple, I sat by the edge of a partly frozen lake. My gaze fell on a number of ducks who would run and then literally skate on the frozen surface - like children! This went on for some time, until I saw them all moving towards a wooden jetty. I soon became aware of the reason. A saffron robed monk was approaching the jetty to feed them! I felt an amazing sense of the connectedness of all things and in all parts of the world.

As a ritual to go within, I have found great stillness in walking a labyrinth which is an ancient pattern, a meditational walking path with one entrance and one path, which twists and circles its snake-like way to the sacred centre. Cedar Prest, OAM, is an Australian artist who works with stained glass. From 2002 to 2003, she was awarded a Churchill Fellowship to pursue newer Art and Health directions and become a Labyrinth Facilitator. She writes, "Walk a labyrinth just once with some preparation from a trained facilitator and you will experience that this is a path of connectedness to your inner soul." Cedar Prest sees her work today as designing and making healing labyrinths especially for aged care facilities, hospitals, hospices, retreat centres and schools. I find that it is a calming and healing thing to do. On a visit to Edinburgh, Scotland, where, as a young nurse, I had completed Part 1 midwifery training at the famous Simpson Memorial Maternity Pavilion, I encountered an open air labyrinth in the old part of the city.

This was a time in my life when I had visited the Island of Iona and been enticed into the Abbey by the sound of a harpsichord. I had also experienced the standing stones of Callanish, found on the Island of Lewis in the Outer Hebrides, Scotland. These stones are 5000 years old, and my mind was beginning to question much about my Christian heritage. Father Richard Rohr writes that Christianity is the "Johnny-come-lately" as compared to Hindu and Buddhist Scriptures, which draw upon inspirations from the collective unconscious or the Eternal One Spirit. In my sixties, I was searching in earnest to find answers to the meaning of life, and I explored many traditions. Because of the Buddhist saying that the state of our mental or spiritual development is the only thing we carry into the next world, I began to meditate daily, to read widely and to have a ritual of saying 'thank you' morning and night, as I light a candle.

The question is, what language to use in religious conversations? For many people traditional religions preaching hellfire and damnation sent messages of fear and guilt. These emotions are seldom helpful in reflecting on their life. For some, the need for confession and absolution is essential. In one instance, the family were extremely grateful when I facilitated a visit from a Catholic priest. The family initially said that such a visit would be the wrong thing to do, as their father never went near a church, although he had been baptised in a Catholic church. What transpired surprised all those at the bedside. The priest visited and gave absolution and a blessing. The man who was dying was scarcely conscious, but as the priest made the sign of the cross, he did also! Intuition played a part in the action of calling a priest, and on reflection I felt it might be more beneficial for the daughter, who was an ardent follower of the Catholic Church, than for her father. The family and friends are all part of end-of-life care and need consideration. The palliative care nurse or team member can imagine a bridge that links the dying person's soul with the next formless, unseen world.

I love learning about the soul! Recently, I learned that the soul speaks to the body and then the body speaks to the mind. Like being aware of your heart pounding, your stomach in knots, a lump in your throat, or a quiver down your spine. We are energy beings and process life through the energy flowing through the body and neural pathways. Reflexology and acupuncture are examples of energy flow through the body. Teilhard de Chardin wrote about a sphere of thought encircling the earth that has emerged through evolution and as a consequence of a growth in consciousness. He called this field of thought the noosphere. He wrote that it is our duty as men and women to proceed as if limits to our ability did not exist and that we are collaborators in creation. Understanding concepts of energy and consciousness highlights the need for a different language to be learned by health providers. Health is not achieved by expecting a doctor or other health professional to make us healthy by considering the body alone. It is our soul's journey; the blockage in energy flow is a reminder to listen to the soul and, through awareness of past and present lives, learn to evolve and increase the level of our vibrations to the vibration of love energy.

Evolution does occur for many through religious observance. Religious observance was beneficial for the dying stage of a very grand lady. She had sent the ambulance away when they responded to a call from those concerned for her health. Nurses cared for her at home and her doctor made home visits. My role was to supervise the situation. Her household staff firmly believed that this very elderly woman knew her own mind and would not want a visit from a priest as she never went to church. A niece felt otherwise, and a visit from a woman priest was organised. It was left for me to convey this pending visit to the patient. I knelt beside the bed and gently said: "You have done everything in life very well and we need to do this part of your life well too. There is an Anglican priest coming to give you a blessing, is that OK?" There were no apparent signs of rejecting the idea, and niece and priest were brought to the bedside. I had requested a blessing and felt a little uncomfortable when the priest invited this matriarch to join in the "Lord's Prayer." We all held hands with the patient and were truly blessed when she voiced all the words with us! She died peacefully several days later.

Conversations regarding the funeral arrangements afford another opportunity to talk about what gives meaning and purpose to a life. I like to talk about the funeral early in the piece and try to justify my doing so with: "It is better to talk about arrangements early, as the emotions which may arise at the time of death tend not to be rational." I am often surprised at the choice of celebrant. For example, a family who have not been active church attendees might seek a celebrant from a religious background for the funeral service, and vice versa. The choice of music and other rituals play a part in uplifting spirits that may have been crushed by loss. It has also been my experience that family members may celebrate the life of the person who has died with a barbecue on the beach, and seem comforted by nature. There is no one way or right way. It is also important to offer choice, and to be an effective advocate for the family. Difficult situations arise when family members disagree. An early discussion can establish the wishes of the person themselves. This is another reason to have an Advance Care Directive. Many of my patients are reluctant to speak about end-of-life preparations and may say: "I have told my lawyer what I want, it is in my will." I explain that a will is not usually read until after death. How the funeral has been conducted is long remembered.

My greatest difficulty in staying in a non-judgemental attitude has been with people who have a narrow and inflexible view of the Bible or other Holy Book's translations. For example: In John 14:6 (NIV), Jesus answered: "I am the way and the truth and the life. No one comes to the Father except through me." Many people interpret these lines as only followers of Jesus go to the heaven of their understanding, rather than appreciating the broader and less literal meaning. Florence Nightingale wrote on ways to unify science and spirituality in order to bring order, meaning, and purpose to human life. She saw Jesus as the man who is already in a state of blessedness, the man who has progressed and succeeded; an example of enlightenment to us rather than someone who saved us. She spoke of the Bible as containing deep truths, but refuted the Scriptures as divine revelation. She also questioned that the Word could be pinned down to either one period or to one church. She described God as a "presence higher than human" and as a divine intelligence that creates, sustains, and organises the universe to which we have an inner connection. She wrote that heaven is neither a place nor a time. Eckhart Tolle writes in *A New Earth* that heaven is not a location but refers to the inner realm of consciousness. Nightingale did not believe that anyone could save a soul except themselves. A Buddhist teaching says:

> *No one saves us but ourselves,*
> *No one can and no one may,*
> *We ourselves must walk the path.*

At one of the Four o'clock Talks I attended in the Shantivanam Ashram in India in 2015, I heard Father John Martin Sahajananda explain this Bible passage. He said that "I am the way, the truth and the life" is the most humble and liberating statement by Jesus, as it encourages followers to adopt his loving nature. Jesus, like Buddha, became an enlightened being and, by his life, showed us the way to the Father or to the Source of all being by becoming conscious of an inner life. In his book *A New Earth*, Eckhart Tolle refers to John 14:6 as the most powerful words uttered by Jesus, if understood correctly. He writes that the very being that you are is Truth, the most innermost "I Am," the essence identity of every man and woman. From a spiritual point of view suffering does not originate in the external world, but as a reaction of the mind to events in life or the external world. Eckhart Tolle's goal is to bring awakened consciousness into the world. The gift of inner knowing without the wrapping of religion. Buddha said:

> Those who have failed to work
> towards the truth
> have missed the purpose
> of living.

I can relate to a "spirit of religion" in my search for a common language to express what we cannot, with our small minds, express. Carolyn Myss, in her book *Entering the Castle: An Inner Path to God and Your Soul*, writes that the New Age isn't new any longer, and, while it opened society to many spiritual traditions and alternative healing methods, it needs to discover the power of intuition, archetypes, and the collective unconscious. C. G. Jung recognised the psyche and unconscious as vehicles for and reflections of the spiritual realm. There is so much to learn in our strivings to be loving presences at the bedside of people who are in the transition from life to death, as well as to fulfill our own destiny.

CHAPTER 6

On Purpose and Meaning

For many from Eastern Traditions, life means karma and reincarnation. Karma, in the classical system of Yoga, can be described as "the way of action." One definition is that karma can be understood as cause and effect, where intent and actions of an individual (cause) influence the future of that individual (effect). More simply, it is the result of our choices. In the Biblical Epistle to the Galatians 6:7, "Be not deceived; God is not mocked: for whatsoever a man soweth, that shall he also reap." It is common for people at the end of life to search the soul for meaning. In *The Tibetan Book of Living and Dying* by Sogyal Rinpoche there is a quote by Origen, one of the most influential of the church fathers in the 3rd century, "Each soul comes to this world reinforced by the victories or enfeebled by the defeats of its previous lives." Those who experience past-life deaths record how that death affects their current life. Christianity eventually rejected reincarnation.

It is the duty of those in the role of caring to have an appreciation of the common threads seen in many religious and spiritual traditions, and to rise above the dogma and divisions to embrace a Oneness with the Source of all or God where there is non-duality; there is no right or wrong, no love or hate, good or bad. God is the Life Force that underpins and connects all - in the plant, animal, human, and cosmic environment: what Dr. Wayne Dwyer referred to as the energy that makes our finger nails grow. He believed that his life purpose was to serve others and teach people how to be self-reliant. He would often be asked, "How do I find my purpose? Does such a thing really exist? Why don't I know my purpose in life?" The last video he made before his death in 2015 focuses on our inner knowing. Bronnie Ware, the inspirational author who wrote, *The Top Five Regrets of the Dying*, identifies how this question of purpose and neglect of the inner knowing (intuition) can affect our lives.

My intuitive awareness accepts that every sensation, every feeling, every imagination, affects my mind and impacts on my soul. Bede Griffiths gives this description of intuition:

> Intuition, then, is the knowledge of the passive intellect, the self-awareness, which accompanies all action and all conscious, deliberate reflection. It is passive: it comes from the world around me, from the sensations of my body, from my feelings and spontaneous reactions. That is why intuition cannot be produced. It has to be allowed to happen. But that is just what the rational mind cannot endure. It wants to control everything. It is not prepared to be silent, to be still, to allow things to happen.

There is so much more to being a midwife to the soul than setting up medications in a syringe driver and being responsive to the result of scientific tests. Many modern-day mystics such as Eckhart Tolle write about being in the Now and about form and formless. As a baby grows, the form changes and expands. In death, the form of the person is shrinking and the functions are ceasing until the formless (or our energetic being, mind, or soul) leaves the body. While it was in the form of a body it grew in many ways; physically, intellectually, emotionally, and spiritually. It responded to the events and circumstances of life. It had the opportunity to be a co-creator with God, and to turn gifts and abilities into full potential or less than their full potential. Perhaps that is why some people say that heaven and hell is here on Earth, and how important it is to listen to the small, still voice of the conscience which speaks with intuitive insights.

Florence Nightingale gave the world a great teaching when she told the people of London to stop praying to God to remove the plague, but rather thank God for showing them that their waterways needed to be cleaned. The spiritual teacher Eckhart Tolle says that we are all confronted with suffering in life and that it is most helpful for spiritual awakening.

His wisdom conveys that it does not originate in the external world but as a reaction of the mind to events in life or the external world. Because suffering arises in the mind it is optional, as we choose our response to thoughts. In end-of-life care what is perceived as suffering has the potential to bring families together, and so have some meaning. Rather than mind perceptions that cause suffering it is helpful to let go of self-absorption and to focus the mind on beauty, such as a sunset or towering mountain peak. Beauty takes many forms and touches all of the senses.

From Islam, the hadith of the Hidden Treasure tells us that God was a hidden treasure who wanted to be known, so He created the world so that He could be known. This gives a cosmic view of creation and the concept of Oneness and evolution. Love is said to be the motivating force of creation. From Rumi, I appreciate that there are many lamps (religions, paths) to shine the way to God, but the light is the same. Another mystical description of enlightenment is said to be when the wave realises it is the ocean. Reflecting on finding meaning and purpose in a lifetime is a state of mind to be shared, especially in the hospice setting. I am aware that the focus of many hospice programs is to promote living to the end, rather than preparing for the end with a spiritual practice.

The bridge between form and formless is energy. Energy can vibrate at difference frequencies and be relentless in stimulation or it can be tranquil and peace promoting. When it is tranquil, the soul has an opportunity to connect to God. My concept of God is to imagine God as a supreme intelligence needing all life (all of us) to manifest or action that intelligence, as archetypical patterns. I also relate to times when we act in harmony with this intelligence and there are times when we 'miss the mark', an expression for sin, taught to me by a friend who is a Catholic nun. A notion is that we co-create with the Divine Masculine Energy and with the Divine Feminine Energy to bring about One. The symbol of Yin and Yang is an example. To do so effectively we need to have a still and receptive mind to hear the subtle voice of intuition.

I cannot accept that everything is driven by the ego and is merely happenstance. While words reduce reality to something the mind can grasp, metaphor and archetype can expand the mind to form a new understanding. An expression I use frequently to describe a person who is near death but becomes energised again is: "Perhaps, it was a dress rehearsal!" In my experience, some people can have many dress rehearsals. Perhaps, in some way, they are preparing the people they love for their departure. This time could be considered anticipatory grief. Grief is a process, and particularly for the person who is preparing to become formless. They are losing all experiences connected with form - a lifetime of experience. Ego and all the things attached to it are a part of form. Some of these parts of ego include thoughts, power, wealth, reputation, and even time.

In 2016, I visited Assisi, and when I think of Saint Francis and his followers, I am reminded of the Saint Francis Prayer:

> Lord, make me an instrument of Your peace. Where there is hatred, let me sow love; where there is injury, pardon; where there is doubt, faith; where there is despair, hope; where there is darkness, light; where there is sadness, joy.

> O, Divine Master, grant that I may not so much seek to be consoled as to console; to be understood as to understand; to be loved as to love; For it is in giving that we receive; it is in pardoning that we are pardoned; it is in dying that we are born again to eternal life.

Father Richard Rohr writes that, like so many Westerners, he grew up knowing almost nothing about Hinduism, even though it is by far the oldest of the Great Religions in the wisdom tradition. He writes that because he had never met a true Hindu, their dress, various gods, and temples seemed so foreign. Hinduism was not taken seriously. He says that it is common to see everything in reference to one's self, whenever one's nationality, era and religion are the only reference points. He writes that Hindu and Buddhist Scriptures draw upon inspirations from the collective unconscious or the Eternal One Spirit. The Hindu and Buddhist belief of reincarnation is reinforced by reading books such as *Destiny of Souls: New Case Studies of Life between Lives* by Michael Newton, PhD and *Life Between Lives* by Brian L. Weiss, MD. These authors used hypnosis to access different states of consciousness in their clients.

Mirabai Starr is another contemporary scholar of philosophy and religion. She writes, speaks and leads retreats on the inter-spiritual teachings of the mystics, and talks about a global spiritual path. In her work, she weaves together the major faiths and talks about mystics having a direct encounter with Spirit, and of wisdom figures lighting her path. She says that the first noble truth of Buddhism can be translated as: "It hurts to be a human and the reason we suffer is because we are wishing things to be different from what they are." In other words, desire, attachment and aversion cause suffering. There is, however, an innate desire for union with God. This brings me to the subject of death, which has been called by Alice Bailey 'The Great Adventure'. Alice Bailey was a writer of more than twenty-four books on theosophical subjects, and was one of the first writers to use the terms New Age and the Age of Aquarius. Death was of interest to the ancient Egyptians, as seen in their legends, symbols and myths. Petra, the famous archaeological site in Jordan's desert, dates back to 300 BCE. For me, what I glean from symbols such as the Tree of Life, the Scarab Beetle, and emblems of royalty and authority, is that the search for Eternal Truths is in my DNA.

As Esoteric Philosophy was a new area for me, I travelled to Brisbane in early March 2016 to attend several days of workshops with William Meader at the Relaxation Centre in Brisbane. William Meader is an international presenter and is one of the most influential teachers of Ageless Wisdom. He lives in Oregon, and presents regular workshops in the United States, Europe, United Kingdom, Canada, Australia, and New Zealand. His book, *Shine Forth: The Soul's Magical Destiny* is well worth reading. Most spiritual traditions teach that we are so much more than our personality and body image, although these attributes contribute to the way we live in the world. In the workshops conducted by William Meader, I learned more about my soul's journey and how, in the language of Esoteric Philosophy, my personality, which is made up of thinking, emotional and physical bodies, needs to fuse with my soul or causal body to become my Higher Self. Esoteric Astrology has become a further tool for self-awareness and assists in a cosmic view point. The word 'shadow', which I was familiar with from a Jungian perspective, was also used by William Meader to demonstrate the distortions of spiritual truth. Then there is destiny and free choice to consider.

For a short period of time, I had a nurse practice in Brisbane as well as Adelaide. This was a very difficult time in my life as my marriage of thirty years was coming to an end. I was seeking answers and understanding. At that time, I was introduced to the Relaxation Centre in Brisbane. This unique organisation was begun in 1974 by two accountants who promoted, with National and International speakers, the power of the mind, the benefits of relaxation, changing attitude and exploring the unconscious. The one resource I still have and value is a recorded session on death and the purpose of life. The presenters are Lionel Fifield (a founder of the Centre), Maryanne Madden (a spiritual healer who has had five near-death experiences) and Dr. James Reid (a medical doctor who aligned himself with the work of Dr. Elisabeth Kubler-Ross). These are some of the helpful insights from this presentation.

First, we suffer little deaths all the time and that dying is a heart function not a brain function. We are souls inhabiting a body along with a spirit, which is the God part of us. Our purpose on Earth is to learn from experiences. Maryanne Madden suggests that we choose the experiences we wish to have before we incarnate. This was also expressed in the Myth of Er before the souls met the three Fates. Life between lives is a time for reflection and evaluation of the events on the physical plane. How one responds to events is a choice and provides an opportunity for reflection on the choice. Experiences are opportunities for becoming a more enlightened individual.

I have often heard the expression: "At birth, you are dealt a hand of cards and it is the way the cards are played that determines your progression along the path to enlightenment." All three presenters agree that it is the state of our mind that we take into the next realm. For example, the mind may be vengeful, angry, guilty, forgiving, loving, compassionate, brave, fearful, understanding, clear, clouded, and so on. I remember hearing at a retreat held at the Ian Gawler Foundation that many people refuse to take opioids for pain relief for fear of losing control of their mind. My feeling is that I need to gain more awareness of the bigger picture of consciousness.

I found it really difficult to understand the word consciousness until I spent three days in the Saccidananda Ashram in Tamilnadu. This Ashram is a leading exponent of Hindu–Christian dialogue. Father Bede Griffiths, who taught in the Ashram until his death in 1993, was a Benedictine monk. His vision was to go beyond religion and the vicious cycle of belief structures to seek a direct union with God. God has many names. I feel God as intuition and personal conscience - we hear and understand the term "clear conscience" as a benchmark for goodness. I also like the idea of co-creating with God. This for me means paying attention to my intuitive thoughts and acting on them to the best of my ability - doing my little bit to make the world more Godlike! I think of consciousness as awareness.

Life is so full of barriers and divisions. There are different religions, different races and cultures, different values, different lifestyles and more. So many writers on the subject of spirituality talk about Oneness. In his book, *The Power of Spiritual Intelligence*, Tony Buzan quotes a Serbian Proverb: "Be humble for you are of the earth. Be noble for you are made of stars." He writes that spiritually intelligent people cultivate an awareness of the magnificence of every living thing and the vast and gigantic beauty of the universe. Many an astronaut's life has been changed by seeing the vastness of Earth. They didn't see the different dogmas, different coloured skins, or different divisive attitudes. Probes exploring space send back photos of our Earth in which it looks like a ball of fire with a thin crust on the surface. It almost looks transparent. As Jean Houston says, "It utterly overwhelms the imagination to consider the size and complexity of our cosmos with its billions of galaxies and trillions of planetary systems, all partaking in the continuous flow of creation."

One day, I visited an elderly, frail woman who, some months before, had moved from living alone to living in residential care. Her memory was sharp and her bright eyes glowed. I introduced myself and asked if she remembered me from being involved with her husband's care. She said very boldly that she not only remembered me but also that I had said, via her daughter, that I had offered her the option of stopping her pills and letting nature take its course. I chuckled and owned the statement. It is an option for elderly people who feel that their time is coming. She added that she was not afraid of dying and was staying alive for her granddaughter, who needed her.

On the next visit, I asked her if she believed in God, and I was told in very definite terms that she prayed every day, and she added that she told her granddaughter to pray too. "We live for each other and she phones every day to see how I am." The granddaughter had been abandoned by her mother at an early age, and the teenage years had been full of strife, including drug induced violence towards the grandmother. This bright spark of a lady believed her purpose in this lifetime was to protect her granddaughter, and even when people advised that she be left to reap the consequences of her actions she proudly and determinedly stuck by her. The pride in achieving her life purpose shone as she prepared for life after death. She told me of her meaningful dreams and visions since she moved into the nursing home. I felt very humble to be in her presence. We need to meet people whose faith, patience, and forgiveness tell us we are still in the kindergarten of love.

"Chapter 2" of the *Bhagavad Gita* writes:

> All beings are invisible before their birth and after death are invisible again. They are seen between two unseens. Why in this find cause for grief?... The spirit that is in all creatures is immortal in them all. Why grieve for death of that which cannot die?

CHAPTER 7

Euthanasia

Euthanatos is a Greek word meaning "good death." The word euthanasia comes from this Greek word, and for many is indeed a word that means good death, and for many others means "mercy killing." When I have been asked if I believe in euthanasia, I have needed to determine which definition of the word is to be considered. Active euthanasia means a deliberate action is taken to cause death, while passive euthanasia is when death is brought by an omission or a withdrawal of treatment. Voluntary euthanasia implies that death is sought with the full knowledge and consent of the patient, while "voluntary active euthanasia" (assisted suicide or physician-assisted dying) is the act carried out by the patient themselves, with the means being provided by another person who has the knowledge of the patient's intentions, and while "non-voluntary euthanasia" implies that the patient does not know that his/her life is being ended; the decision is being made by another person. Those descriptions seems to be soul denying and, for me, they are not very helpful for a soul who knows that it is time to leave the physical form. What is needed is sacred activism for those who are facing the end of their life. By this, I mean that the end of the physical body is a matter for the soul rather than a medical matter.

As of January 2016, human euthanasia is legal only in the Netherlands, Belgium, Ireland, Colombia, and Luxembourg. Assisted suicide is legal in Switzerland, Germany, Japan, Albania, and Canada; and in the US states of Washington, Oregon, Vermont, New Mexico, Montana, and California. Assisted suicide or physician-assisted dying is mainly for grievous and irremediable medical conditions. It is a debate that causes emotionally charged arguments from organised religions to the most studied fields of bioethics. I do not wish to enter into a debate, but to share how I feel about my time to face death. Most people who are facing the end of their life because of disease or age do not find it easy to die. Eastern traditions such as Hinduism, and particularly Buddhism, as well as shamanic traditions, have explicit teachings that guide the dying to a conscious and graceful death. A change in attitude is needed for death to be offered as a choice to a person who is nearing the end of their life.

> Death is only evil when it is seen from the point of view of the ego – the ego which is enclosed in itself and refuses to die, to surrender itself to God. When the self is surrendered to God, then death becomes a sacrament; it is simply the passage into eternal life.
> —Spiritual Master, Bede Griffiths

When contemplating physician-assisted dying there are three important considerations, which concern relationships. First, there is the relationship the person has with their soul or inner dimension. Second, there is the relationship with their families. Families are formed by birth, marriage, work environment, sporting teams, and spiritual communities of many kinds. Third, there is the relationship with their Higher Power (by whatever name this energy is called). All decisions involve the concept of karma and the wheel of life. Death is more than a doorway - it is a threshold to a higher level of consciousness. Many writers refer to a life review at this time. Others refer to the interconnectedness of all of humanity. I see this interconnectedness in a spider's web, which is sensitive to the entrapment of a small insect in one corner being felt in the whole. The person who requests physician-assisted dying needs to be aware of these compound affects, not only on people who are alive today but on generations to come.

While hospices and the practice of palliative care have improved the way people with terminal illness die, there are many elderly people who seem to live in a state of medicated limbo in our aged care facilities who do not qualify for these programs. When presenting to nursing home staff, I would often say that there need to be Achievement Boards in the rooms where elderly are cared for. These Achievement Records, along with positive death talk, could go some way to making the elderly person so content with their life experience that they have the confidence to leave this plane of existence.

Erik Erickson, the developmental psychologist, best known for his theory on the "Eight Stages of Man," wrote that healthy children will not fear life if their elders have integrity enough not to fear death. To my mind, it is a question of ceasing to rely on life-prolonging pharmaceuticals and allowing nature to take its course when I can no longer care for the body which has housed my soul. I may need to request medication in the process of shedding my worn out body. In my experience, a person who calmly anticipates death may choose to hold a final farewell celebration. I met one courageous elderly man who chose the time of death. A month prior, he invited all his friends to a lunch at his club.

I see death as a spiritual event and the transition of the soul from this physical world to the world of spirit or formlessness from where it came. My guiding force is my inner voice, and I do not view my death as a medical or political problem, but rather as a soul journey. As one of my Catholic nun friends says: "Death is a terminus where the soul gets off one bus only to board another." There needs to be a consideration of a person's belief about life, life's purpose, and whether their belief extends to more than a physical body, which simply returns to dust. Who is the best person to assist another to clarify their beliefs? I began with a chapter on reincarnation, which is my belief. Florence Nightingale wrote:

> As each individual embodies unique qualities that cannot be duplicated, it would not be consistent with God's benevolent nature to obliterate that being. Because it is God's plan to raise mankind from imperfection to perfection, death must initiate a different mode of existence, one that allows for continued development.

I have enjoyed listening to the songs, as well as reading about the life, of the French cabaret singer Edith Piaf. Her varied experiences in life included being brought up in a brothel and enjoying world fame, even singing in the iconic Carnegie Hall. She took her own life when she could no longer sing and move audiences with her songs. She lived her life with unbridled passion and attracted many lovers. Lifestyle played a part in shortening her life.

Many people shorten their life through lifestyle choices, which may include tobacco, stress, and harmful drugs. Yet stories abound of a loving spouse or child shortening the life of a person with a terminal illness with an overdose of prescribed medication to relieve pain and suffering. The penalties given by the law of the land for such actions are frequently severe. The question to consider is: was the intention of the action a loving one? Or was it evil and self-serving? An intention is in the heart and difficult to discern. If the action is not for the common good, what is appropriate punishment in this world? Choosing to die when terminally ill is not the same as committing suicide in a moment of depression and despair. What factors influence a decision to delay or postpone death with the use of medical science and technology? I have seen the administration of oxygen prolong the bedside vigil, as well as artificial feeding. There are many factors to consider, and many questions without clear answers.

The image of a dying person tied to a bed with feeding tubes in place is more disturbing to me than starvation. This is especially distressing when the body naturally withdraws from food and fluids as part of the dying process. This suffering was seen when I went to see one of my patients who had kept a routine appointment at a major teaching hospital. The elderly woman was bravely living her last days with a brain tumour. She had discharged herself from a small private hospital to a motel where she could see boats. Her home was in a coastal town and she had a boat of her own. As she was not able to go to her real home she settled for a motel near the hospital. One of my carers stayed with her to assist with her care. Her speech was becoming affected, as was her balance. She planned to take a week-long river cruise with a very good friend. The planning included a chauffeur driven car to make the seventy-kilometer journey. We talked about her wishes, and she made it very clear that when there was no quality in her life she didn't want to be here. She did appreciate the small caring touches of having a manicure and her hair washed and set.

The week on the cruise was difficult; the return trip was made in an ambulance. When I went to visit her in hospital I found her hands tied to bedrails, an intravenous infusion going into her arm. A feeding tube was in her nose and the nurse was about to give her an enema. She looked at me with frantic pleading eyes. She could not talk, but she kept leaning forward and with her restrained hand gesturing that she wanted to cut her throat. I told the nurse that the treatment was not the patient's wish and asked for a doctor in authority who could order a palliative care approach. I constantly ask the question: "Whose needs are we meeting?" After some delay, a doctor came and formalised her discharge back to the small private hospital where she had been admitted before her time on the cruise boat. Pain-relieving medication was also ordered and the patient was transferred back to her private hospital. Once there I found her almost in a coma. I asked if I had done the right thing by speaking up for her. The reply was a contented yawn!

The legislation that encourages a person to make an Advance Care Directive goes a little way in allowing futile treatment to be ceased or not commenced. More honest conversations are being had. Yet making an Advance Care Directive is a small first step. When the time comes to act on an Advance Care Directive and adopt a palliative care approach, fear of death can be palpable among those making the decision. In a discussion about death and dying with a woman in her nineties, I remember saying that there is a strong survival gene in the ego, and that the ego needed to die for a peaceful death to take place. The next day this woman phoned me to ask what it was that she had 'to kick aside' so that she could die. With a smile, I reminded her of the survival gene in her ego. I have experienced several patients who had the courage to die consciously. One former nurse commented that her fingernails were becoming blue as the peripheral circulation was shutting down. Another woman while sitting on the toilet started to cough. She asked, looking me in the eye, if these coughs were the death rattle. I replied, "Not yet!"

A case that filled my heart with pride was when a retired medical specialist asked me to be in charge of his dying. This man with many heart problems was at home among the eucalyptus trees that surrounded his home and being cared for mainly by his loyal and devoted wife. They had spent the night together in the bed they had shared for many years. During the night, the doctor warned his wife several times that his life was fading and, in the early morning, summoned me to his bedside. He said, "I'm dying, and I want you to be in charge." I was shocked by his pragmatic attitude and asked him if he could wait until his son arrived from interstate that evening. The atmosphere in the home was peaceful, much like waiting for a birth. At noon, the GP arrived on a Harley-Davidson motorbike in his leathers, and prescribed pain relief and sedation.

The patient was clean, the bed linen was fresh, hands were held and stories told. Birds sang in the treetops. The sons arrived, but still there was no last breath. The patient seemed to be enjoying it all, but the family and nurse were becoming weary. This is not uncommon, and it can be quite stressful when a family prepare for the event of death and then it is slow to happen. I would remind those in the vigil that we have time to catch up on our rest, and that this is the time for those preparing to leave. In contrast, imagine a person who feels that their only course of action is to take the lonely road of unassisted dying. Do existing laws against assisted dying prolong life, or rather, cruelly prolong death?

Autonomy is very important to many people. In the early days of my practice, I would meet elderly women who let me know that they had their supply of special pills. I would not discourage the conversation, but recall only one person who took them. I write about it my book, *As Good As Goodbyes Get: A Window into Death and Dying*. In certain instances, palliative care doctors are permitted to order terminal sedation as long as the intention is for pain relief and not to hasten death. What does it mean to "do no harm", which is a tenet of ethical argument? Many so-called beneficial therapies also have serious risks and side-effects. The pertinent ethical issue is whether the benefits outweigh the burdens. I would often ask families of loved ones who were dying, what can you live with? Can you live with sanctioning treatment that may prolong life but also prolong suffering? These difficult dilemmas are many and varied, and highlight the second relationship, which is with others. It is helpful if the patient makes their personal wishes and beliefs known, so that family members are in agreement and not carrying the heavy energy of regret with them for the rest of their lives.

Richard Lamerton, a palliative care physician from the United Kingdom, teaches that the role of the palliative care team is to make the body a comfortable enough place to live in while the person prepares to die, if that is their wish. Sogyal Rinpoche says that one of the chief reasons we have so much anguish and difficulty facing death is that we ignore the truth of impermanence. We so desperately want everything to continue as it is. Yet the timing of the last breath is a mystery. Dying people do seem to have a say about when to take that last breath. Consider the retired medical specialist's death. He was dying consciously while the medications used in palliative care enabled his body to relax. There was no tension, just peace. I thought he could have died before the doctor came at midday, but he knew that his sons were on their way and I intuited that he chose to wait for them. This is a common story in hospice care. I have often said that it doesn't seem to matter what medications we give, the soul energy seems to leave the body when it is ready or directed by unseen influences.

I learned the lesson of impermanence when I visited my father's farm many years after his death. I found that trees and grass had reclaimed the showcase pineapple farm. A Buddhist friend comforted me by reminding me of impermanence. He said that the farm had been my father's work while he was on Earth and reminded me of the intricate sand mandalas the Buddhist monks make and then pour into a river to demonstrate impermanence. Back to euthanasia. If a person feels deeply that their time on Earth has served its purpose and they wish to "go home," I do not think health professionals and the law need to be obstructive. Asking to go home is a common request by people in a secured dementia ward. Yet they are weighed, fed high protein drinks, and treated for other medical conditions in an effort to maintain the life of the physical body. Families have a say in care, and so many seem to project their own health needs and fear of death onto these sad cases. Like the people in the allegory of Plato's cave, education is surely the key to enlightenment and comprehension.

I feel that the key to choosing the time for the physical body to die is choice. It is written in many Holy Texts that God gave man free will. Death is not an easy decision but when it has been the choice made by one of my patients following a process of discernment, I have respected the decision and coordinated appropriate palliative care support. My mantra has been that a good death is one where the heart is filled with a love of life rather than a "poor me" attitude. End-of-life conversations are difficult for many people, including those in the caring profession, and for many reasons. Death may have been a taboo subject in many families for fear of a family member being misunderstood if the topic is raised. Yet, most elderly people appreciate honest, non-judgemental opportunities to reflect on their life and to feel that there will be a midwife or medical person to see them through the dying process. The Buddhist approach is expressed in the following is written by Venerable Pende Hawter, who I first knew as a Queensland physiotherapist and later as a Buddhist monk active in the palliative care movement.

> Because the way in which we live our lives and our state of mind at death directly influence our future lives, it is said that the aim or mark of a spiritual practitioner is to have no fear or regrets at the time of death. People who practice to the best of their abilities will die, it is said, in a state of great bliss. The mediocre practitioner will die happily. Even the initial practitioner will have neither fear nor dread at the time of death. So one should aim at achieving at least the smallest of these results.

This statement is a guideline for all those working with people at the end of their life. Imagine having no fear or regret at the time of death! This is a difficult goal to attain if the medical model of dying with designated pathways is the only guide. Leaving this Earth, for me, is a personal responsibility and involves facing the dark aspects of myself that I need to reconcile, release, or heal. It is my passion to respect people's informed and heartfelt choices, and to listen respectfully to their intuitive guidance. When it comes to care givers desiring to give the best possible care to a dying person, I cannot speak highly enough of the *Tibetan Book of Living and Dying* written by Sogyal Rinpoche and edited by Patrick Gaffney and Andrew Harvey. Obviously, there will be different levels of consciousness, beliefs, and values, not only among those who are dying but also among family, friends, and care givers. I feel this is what Dr. Elisabeth Kubler-Ross meant when she advised that care be given with a non-judgemental attitude and with love. All care that supports those in the process of dying needs to be given mindfully and from a heart-space of stillness and love.

Florence Nightingale wrote that the purpose of a lifetime was to come from imperfection to perfection, and that it needed more than one lifetime to achieve this aim. This may be of some comfort to those who experience death by suicide. From my readings on life after death, a form of learning for the soul, at different levels or realms, continues. Florence Nightingale wrote that she didn't believe in a punitive God, but rather one who was like an earthly father who still loved his children even when their behaviour did not please. All the major religions believe in a life after death. Suicides occur for many reasons, and some are accidental, following the taking recreational drugs. Mostly, depression is the cause of suicide, and a Pagan explanation is that a death from depression can be seen as the wheel of life, which travels through the seasons and from sadness into joy being stuck. The person is out of balance and sees only despair. Just as each soul journey is individual, so will the solution for a depressed person be individual.

This chapter is titled "Euthanasia," and there are many factors to consider when evaluating what constitutes a good death. To quote William Meader: "As a teacher of the Esoteric Spiritual Philosophy, my goal is to promote the spiritual journey and the evolution of the human consciousness." For some, this will mean a disciplined spiritual practice and a thirst for the sacred. Everyone, it seems, is given something to endure in a lifetime. This may be called karma by those who believe in Eastern philosophies. Others may relate to the image of a sword needing to go through fire in the process of strengthening. There are many life events to test a person's faith. One hears of a person being on 'the path,' which implies that there is a spiritual component to earthly life, and a process of life evaluation. Carolyn Myss writes that self-examination is the practice of becoming your truth. In the introduction, I detailed some of the tools I have used while striving to become my truth. In addition, I spent thirty hours experiencing hypnosis with a medical doctor who said that this was equivalent to three years of psychotherapy! The concept of knowing my conscious and unconscious self and finding my special task or calling has energised my life.

I recall talking to a family member who was dying. I told this relative the story, which I heard at a Nurse Healers' Conference in New York many years ago. The story is about Milton Erickson, who has been called the father of modern hypnosis. Erickson was raised in a farming community in Wisconsin. The story told of Erickson finding a lost horse and somehow taking him to the rightful owner. When the owner asked Erickson how he knew to bring the horse to him, Erickson replied: "I didn't. All I did was keep him on the road and he knew his own way home." When I finished telling my relative this powerful metaphor he said: "When I was a boy my father was a milkman who made deliveries with a horse and cart. I would sometimes travel with him. As the milk round was finishing my father used to give the horse free rein and we both went to sleep while the horse took us home." I have often said that the person who is dying doesn't need to be awake for the soul's journey to continue, and I recognise the place of sedation in palliative care.

There are many distractions to living a life of purpose and being of service to fellow travellers on the journey. There is a saying among hospice workers that the concern is not an addiction to morphine but to the hospice itself. It has been a challenge to stay with my addiction to caring for people at a time of life that reveals the authentic self. During difficult stressful times, I tried unsuccessfully to abort my passion for promoting the profession of nursing and caring for those who were dying. The difficulties of running a fee for service nurse practice were often overwhelming. Dr. Elisabeth Kubler-Ross said that people suffering from cancer were the lucky ones as they received, without question, excellence in end-of-life care. My heart goes out to those who are dying slowly from age. There is so much more that can be done to relieve their emotional and spiritual pain. Yet, to do this, nurses and doctors need to find a more effective language for end-of-life conversations and for implementing the sentiments expressed in the patient's Advance Care Directive.

It is my belief that death needs to be a legal choice for those who, in their soul, feel it is their time to graduate from a physical body that can no longer support their overall needs for meaning and purpose, comfort and peace of mind. The secret of a good death, I have read, is to die with a love of life. My feeling is that most people facing this profound life event appreciate assistance in some form, just as assistance is appreciated at birth. Those health professionals who support people who are dying need to actively engage in the process of dying in a soul supporting way. They may have a morning greeting that goes something like this: "I see you are still with us. Is there anything keeping you here that we can assist with?" All relationships need honest and trustworthy communication.

CHAPTER 8

Healing Invisible Wounds

My divorce at the age of fifty-four left children and their parents wounded. I knew deep down that I had soul work to do in this life time and that I needed to be myself to do this work. When my husband told me that he wasn't going to support my palliative care nurse practice, I replied that I was not going to stop the work that I had begun. Looking back, I felt called to do this work and, in spite of not being supported by the traditional medical and nursing professions, I knew that ocean waves from behind me were pushing my small wave relentlessly towards the shore of destiny. Looking back, there were many unseen hands to guide me. One of the first was to direct me into a commercial stream of study, where I learned keyboard skills and bookkeeping. Training to be a nurse exposed me to both life and death. Travel introduced me to different cultures and different world views. Through the eyes of my children, I saw my own childhood struggles, challenges and gifts. My marriage in the Catholic Church taught me the best and worst of organised religion. My grandchildren demonstrate the progress they are making through having freedom of thought and a love of life.

Healing invisible wounds is about forgiveness, seeing events through a clear unbiased lens and grieving. This healing, for me, is facilitated by revisiting old photographs, carefully kept greeting cards, books that beg to be reread and by bringing to mind the people who gave me a sense of something greater than the visible world. Intuition has always been a strong guiding voice, even when it was not welcomed. Looking after my mother for the last weeks of her life was a wakeup call. I recognised the genuine caring to be found in those who lived simple lives and yet enjoyed and respected nature. I recognised aspects of others' souls that made me feel at home in their company. I also began to recognise people's energy, and in particular the energy patterns that did not make me feel comfortable or good. With more sensitivity to energy, I became more discerning of energy that I attracted or repelled. I became aware of the influence of past lives and the sacred contract I seemed to have made before I was born. I have reflected on the fairy stories and myths that claim my attention and wonder about the personal myth that I seem to be weaving.

Most importantly, I became more and more aware of the energy centres called chakras and their role in my physical, emotional, and spiritual wellbeing. For me, they provide a template for healing wounds associated with the characteristics of each energy field. For example, the base chakra represents the tribe or culture we were born into in a particular lifetime. As our soul journey unfolds, there will be times when we outgrow or disagree with our birth tribe. I know I did. I grew up in a very religious household. My parents were most fervent followers of the Methodism. They practiced their religion by saying Grace before each meal and, after breakfast, would read from a book for *Daily Devotions* which featured a Bible reading followed by a commentary. On Sundays, the whole family would attend an afternoon church service, which would follow Sunday School for children. My father taught in Sunday School, and as a lay preacher when required. My mother played the church organ and encouraged singing of hymns in the tradition favoured by Charles Wesley the founder of the Methodist Church.

Other meetings were held in the small country church, such as Christian Endeavour and Harvest Thanksgiving, when a large array of fruit, flowers and other produce would be displayed on the raised platform which supported the pulpit. Missionaries would be supported in overseas countries; this support included sending money, books, and clothing. Members of the church would be invited to promise a proportion of their income to the work of the local church as well as other branches of the Church. Synods or ecclesiastical governing or advisory council meetings were attended regularly by my parents. Visiting evangelists would be welcomed and meetings well attended. Best clothes were worn to church activities, and Sunday School picnics were special events. No work was done on a Sunday and sport was not played, it was a "day of rest and worship."

I began to question what I had been raised to believe when I attended a boarding school and met friends from other walks of life and religions. Even before boarding school, I questioned the need for the lack of activity on a Sunday, which seemed unnatural for a child. I would be embarrassed by my father's insistence on saying Grace before each meal, even if we were guests in a home which did not have this habit. I was unhappy as a child when I could not attend the dances held in the school. I loved the music and slippery floor, not encouraged in case these natural instincts might lead to sin. Alcohol was forbidden, and as children we were encouraged to sign the pledge saying that we would never drink alcohol. The same prohibition applied to gambling in all forms. I was sensitive to the fact that not all religions had the same rules and that people who had a different beliefs such as the Catholic Church were not allowed to attend the church activities my parents organised.

When I attended a private school in the city, I could see no harm in playing sport on a Sunday or in a moderate consumption of alcohol. I liked the friends who had different values to those of my parents, and felt the need to make my own decisions on how to live my life. As a young adult, I still felt the need to attend church, but felt more comfortable attending an Anglican service, and liked reading poems written by Gerard Manly Hopkins, who was an English poet and Jesuit priest in the Victorian era. Perhaps my rebellion could be seen when I married a Catholic man who was, in many ways, the opposite of my father. My search for the meaning and purpose of life was strengthened by thirty years of working as a nurse with people who were dying, by travels to different countries and by taking an interest in cultural and world affairs. It became important for me to heal my relationships with my birth tribe in order to move into a chosen future.

Healing my base chakra was just a beginning, and over the years, I have reflected on the other main chakras, while applying the principles of healing by releasing and forgiving myself and others.

There were also times in my role as a palliative care nurse when I needed to be grounded in order to relate to those families in my care. While we are all in different stages of conscious awareness, there are emotions common to all. These are some practical suggestions for grief:

Physical

- It is easy to neglect yourself when you are grieving, and physical symptoms are many.
- Smile and reinforce your self-worth in the many areas of your life with a daily mantra practice.
- Exercise in nature if possible. You may need to feel alone or you may seek company
- You may be more susceptible to illness, as stress has an adverse effect on the immune system. Live as mindfully as possible.
- Try to eat healthy food, even if you find little enjoyment in eating.
- Although sleep may be disturbed, try to get adequate rest while listening to your choice of music.
- It is healthy to cry; tears are the sprinkler system of the soul and release endorphins
- If you have specific symptoms see your doctor without delay.
- Take the advice of trusted friends regarding your health and well-being, as emotions may prevent a rational assessment of your symptoms.

Social

- Friends and family are often most available early in bereavement and less so later. It is important to be able to reach out to them when you need them - don't wait for them to guess your needs. Be true to yourself and others. Accepting support can be difficult.
- During a period of grief it can be difficult to judge new relationships. It is wise not to try to fill an aching void with a new closeness while still holding feelings for the person who has died. More pain may result if you, unconsciously, project the feelings you had for the person who has died onto another person.
- Try to make it clear to children that sadness is perfectly normal and is felt when there is a loss of someone who has been loved.

Early lessons are learned with the loss of a pet. A ritual around the death can be helpful. Buying another one does not replace the feelings for the pet that has died any more than adults pursuing a relationship in haste.

In General

- Avoid hasty decisions. Try not to make major life decisions while grieving. Grief takes many twists and turns. The person who has died will be missed in many ways. At the time of death there can be a sense of relief that the suffering is over. However, the role the deceased person played, as well as the relationship, will take time to grieve.
- Seek wisdom in decision making from trusted family and friends - especially in regard to major financial decisions.
- Heal the past with forgiveness so that you can move into the future. Express, rather than repress, feelings.
- Avoid using busyness to put grief on hold. It is about balance. There is a time for grief with all its loneliness and disbelief, and a time to put grief on hold in order to attend to the activities of living. This may include a job to be kept, a garden to water, children to be care for and bills to be paid.
- Above all, befriend you Higher Self for guidance and understanding.
- You may experience an awareness of the person who has died, and a connection through one of the senses or in a dream.

I came from a simple life on a pineapple farm, yet feel comfortable with people who come from a higher status in society. I have had the opportunity and drive to visit many parts of the world, yet it is inspiration that comes in the quiet moments of listening for guidance that keeps me involved with my fellow travellers. Wounds are connected with pain. Pain can be suppressed, but needs to be resolved before the pain diminishes. This can be seen when medication lowers a person's resolve not to bring wounds to the surface, in an effort to avoid the pain associated with the wounds. Many people go into their next life with unresolved grief or stuck energy patterns. Grief is an emotion felt in the body. Feelings are recognised in the mind. These feelings may include anxiety, apprehension, shame, stress, fear, guilt, empathy, hopelessness, frustration, overwhelm, sadness, happiness and excitement. Emotions are felt in the body and may be experienced as a nervous tummy, difficulty in breathing, sweaty palms, trembling legs, tears, headache, nausea, backache, muscles spasms, smiles and frowns. Father Richard Rohr puts it this way:

> The mind wants a job and believes that its job is to process things by its own criteria. The key to stopping this obsessive game is, quite simply, peace, silence, or stillness.

> One of the signs of non-dual consciousness is that you can actually understand and be patient with dualistic thinkers, even though you can no longer return to that straightjacket yourself. The many individuals who have charted the development of consciousness all agree that the lower levels are dualistic and the higher levels become more and more non-dual. The non-dual mind is open to everything. It is capable of listening to the other, to the body, to the heart, to all the senses. It begins with a radical "yes" to each moment.

Feelings are not dualistically right or wrong, they are just feelings at a particular time. They do need to be expressed (like expressing a pimple full of pus) for healing to take place. For end - of - life care to be meaningful and healing it needs to support people with the safe expression of their feelings. Many of these feelings will have been long buried in the unconsciouss, but will be triggered by an outside influence such as a movie, story, picture, or piece of music. What is helpful to this preparation for death is to have a trusted and "in the present moment" listener. The listener needs to be sensitive to the emotions which have been listed and are felt in the body. Tears are not difficult to associate with sadness. Other emotions such as nausea or backache may need deeper probing.

In the book *Heal Your Mind* by Mona Lisa Schulz and Louise Hay, charts are given to illustrate how to connect a health problem with the emotional situation that may have given rise to it. One of the charts uses the chakras and their representation as a guide. Another chart names a Problem and its Probable Cause as well as giving a New Thought Pattern, which may be beneficial. For example, the Problem of bad breath has the Probable Cause of anger and revenge thoughts and of experiences backing up. The New Thought Pattern is given as "I release the past with love. I choose to voice only love." Another condition listed under the heading of Problem is constipation. A Probable Cause is listed as "refusing to release old ideas. Stuck in the past. Stinginess." New Thought Pattern which is given: "As I release the past, the new and fresh and vital enter. I allow life to flow through me."

While the concept of a mind and body connection was still new to me, I remember being asked to look after a woman in her nineties who was almost blind. She lived alone and refused to leave her own home, which she had adapted with markers of one kind and another. I remember the blanket on her bed had a safety pin to indicate the bottom of the blanket. It also marked the centre of the blanket to ease the making of the bed. As well as dressing an ulcer on her leg, her main concern was constipation. She would insist on having an enema, although the result showed that it probably wasn't necessary. I remember connecting this request to a feeling that this woman needed to get all that did not serve her out of her life in preparation for death, and probably said as much in a joking way.

A bond between us did develop, and late one afternoon I felt the need to visit her. I found her quite breathless with a clammy skin. She said she knew I would come. I told her that we needed to call her doctor. He confirmed heart failure and ordered medication to keep her comfortable. I agreed to stay with her as she rejected the suggestion that hospital care was needed. She died just after midnight in her own bed, as was her wish. I realise what a privilege it has been to be able to offer those in my care flexible and patient-centred care. The GP came the next morning to attend to the paper work. We both felt good about the support we had given this elderly lady who, in her own way, prepared to die.

Invisible wounds are many and varied and affect future generations. From my studies with Thomas Hubl, I find it helpful to see life as a flow or river of energy. There are times and places when this flow of life energy alters course, flowing smoothly and swiftly, and at other times is an eddy stuck on a circular path. There are times when fear and anxiety cause the person in this stream to clutch at overhanging branches and resist going forward. This sensation is commonly found in people who are facing the end-of-life in an unexamined and unguided way. Letting go of these branches and going with the flow of life takes courage and faith. Such courage includes embracing new ideas and new technology. For me, it means embracing energy medicine and supporting practitioners who work in this valuable area.

Grief is a response to loss, and loss includes: loss of self-esteem, loss of relationship, loss of possessions and loss of country, as well as loss by death. Healing comes by changing a belief. Louise Hay says that life is very simple - what we give out we get back! In her book, she gives examples of the many messages we received as children that did not serve our highest good. She writes that when we grow up, we have a tendency to re-create the emotional environment of our early home life. She gives the example of a father or mother who did not know how to love themselves, and states that it would have been impossible for them to teach their children to love themselves. The victim archetype is common to all, according to Caroline Myss. This means that we are all victims of victims, a difficult cycle to break without becoming conscious of the memory. I was with a man in his sixties who said after his mother had taken her last breath, "She still didn't tell me that she loved me." This is the real work of hospice - healing invisible wounds. However, it is incumbent on all those who work with people facing the end of their life to heal their own invisible wounds before attempting to heal the wounds of another.

CHAPTER 9

Connecting Deeply and Mindfully

Bede Griffiths is the Benedictine monk who went to India to discover the other half of his soul and to live out his days in an Ashram, which incorporated Christianity and Hindu ways of living and thought. This is recorded in his book *The Marriage of East and West*. He states that the final stage in human growth is reached when the human consciousness goes beyond its natural limits, beyond the categories of time and space, and encounters the consciousness of the One (energy stream that connects all life). He also writes that in meditation we transcend the categories of space and time and experience this one reality. Can we imagine a time when the practice of meditation would be a daily activity in our health care settings? Maybe the day will come when a nurse will say to a patient: "I've come to take you to the shower, and on the way let us both concentrate on our breathing and nothing else."

The following quote from Deepak Chopra is in response to the deep saying: "I Am That."

> "That" is the steady state of awareness that doesn't change even as thoughts and feelings come and go. At the movies, we focus on the flickering images that tell a story, but without a screen to project them on to, there can be no story. In the same way, without the steady state of awareness, our life stories cannot unfold.

Psychologist and mindfulness meditation teacher Jon Kabat-Zinn has simply defined mindfulness with these words: "...paying attention in a particular way: on purpose, in the present moment, and non-judgmentally."

What sounds simple is often very difficult to achieve. I remember one instance when, in the middle of my busy office, a carer brought a patient who suffered from dementia for a visit. I am aware that people remember you by the way you make them feel, so I tried to make all my patients feel special. I greeted this woman with "How nice to see you! You used to be... (mentioned her maiden name, which was noteworthy) and you used to play tennis." She beamed and walked over to the table where we shared a cup of tea. I had produced my late mother's best Shelley china cups and saucers, knowing that they would be appreciated on some level by our visitor. The carer and I held our breath while this dear little lady, who could become quite agitated, proceeded with shaking hands to carry the cups and saucers some distance to wash and dry them. This simple act encouraged me to live in the moment and to stay very still and focused. The reward was a beaming smile from a normally agitated person. The state of the individual carer's energy impacts on those receiving care.

I developed a habit of using Reiki signs as a form of prayer while driving to visit a patient. Therapeutic Touch taught me "to centre," which is a form of being in the present moment. The effect of not being in the present moment was demonstrated in a class situation by an Australian palliative care nurse, Molly Carlile AM, who describes herself as the Death talker. Molly had us work in pairs, and for one person to be the nurse who was admitting a new resident to a nursing home and the other person to be the new resident. There were standard type questions to ask. The first test was for the interviewer, following the asking of a question, to be busy counting in one's head while the interviewee responded. This was compared to the experience of listening to answers with full and undivided attention. The interviewee was to comment on how each approach made them feel. Obviously, the first method lacked connection, and did not make the person feel valued.

I experienced a non-mindful connection at first hand when I was meeting a new patient and taking a history. I had just been studying on a counselling course the different types of questions used by people in caring professions to obtain information. While asking my questions, my mind pondered whether my questions were direct or indirect questions, rather than on the replies to my questions. Not surprisingly, the patient chose a different nursing service! Having mindful interactions is a basic requirement for all health professionals if they genuinely seek to connect with those in their care. This may be done with the breath or with loving touch.

Perhaps my most mindful moments came at the bedside of a person who was dying. At that time, my attention was focused on general comfort and positioning of the patient. It was also a time to pay attention to the needs of the patient's family and friends. If they are distressed in anyway or fearful of the process of dying, this ruffled energy will intrude on the patient and the soul's preparations. For creating a peaceful atmosphere, strategies may include playing soft music and "remembering when" conversations, as well as praise for relationships and contributions. Life needs to hold meaning in whatever way makes sense to the person who is dying.

My role as a palliative care nurse was multifaceted. In the home environment it is easier to find prompts to draw attention to. These may include photographs, trophies and souvenirs, paintings, books on the bookshelf, or the state of the garden. In mindful conversations, a connection at a deeper level can be made. One patient remarked when he became bedbound that he was surprised by my gentleness (my healer archetype). He had previously only seen in me my duchess archetype, which he admitted made him feel secure. Understanding personal archetypes and the role they play is another essential component of effectively supporting a person who is dying. My strong advocate archetype was able to speak up for patients when they could no longer speak for themselves.

Mindfulness at the bedside is being a loving presence who is not thinking about a previous dilemma or what has to be done before a certain time. It is suspending judgement on past events and resisting the need to plan ahead. A profound moment occurs with the person's last breath. Perhaps this is why so many who have been significant in the person's life express the wish to be present for that moment. Sometimes the moment has been marked with a circle of holding hands by those present, a minute's silence, the Lord's Prayer. Whatever the impulse, it is a moment to put emotions and thoughts on hold and to accept what *is* in the fullness of the moment. A friend of mine, Cedar Prest, designs glass labyrinths that can be traced with a finger when walking a labyrinth is no longer possible or practical. The intention is to go within, to the eternal stillness, for guidance before returning to the outside world. Spiritual Director, Peggy Rubin, writes that medieval pilgrims gave it a different meaning. If unable to make the sacred journey to Jerusalem or Mecca, they could walk the labyrinth with the same intention, and achieve equal spiritual merit.

I encouraged family and those present to assist in the after death ritual of washing and dressing the body of the person who had just died. So many have thanked me for this final intimacy. I loved to add touches of perfume or aftershave and to put fresh flowers in the room, as well as tiding away all signs of illness. I would like to support the closed mouth with a small box, lipstick holder, or the inside cardboard roll from a toilet roll, and wrap the prop in a cravat, scarf, or handkerchief. A favourite rug or bedspread to cover the bed might have added an individual touch. I liked to leave a salt lamp or a candle burning. If a smoke alarm could be set off I have used an electric candle. Mostly, there was an awareness of love and peace that cannot be described. All items of nursing equipment would be cleared away, as well as the clothing and slippers. Chairs would be placed by the bedside for those who wished to spend time in this sacred space where thoughts were the vehicles for communication. There was usually no rush to hurry the body away.

Yes, there were occasions of painful emotions such as grief and even anger arising, but the simple act of sharing a cup of tea or a glass of wine mindfully, in the moment, went some way to beginning the process of healing. Phone calls did need to be made and the funeral people arranged but in a calm, mindful way. Planning the funeral is another activity best done in a mindful way. Photographs for a memorial DVD and music for the service may need to be selected. Special people need to be chosen for other meaningful tasks, such as the eulogy and refreshments. Mainly, I found that a favourite nightdress or pyjamas were chosen to dress the person's body prior to leaving the house, but sometimes a dress or suit from a special occasion such as a wedding would be chosen by the family. Another mindful moment is when the funeral people take away the person's body. Some people request that this happens via the main door rather than a side or back door and, proudly some form a guard of honour. One grieving widow placed her husband's well-worn hat on his covered body as he was taken away from the house for the last time. This transfer was timed for after school so that grandchildren were able to participate in the ritual.

Touching moments abounded. It was not for me to judge people's choices or how, indeed, they grieved. One man whose wife I had cared for told me that he had been warned about the casserole ladies that would be calling, perhaps with a special friendship or relationship in mind. I saw on some occasions that a widower would form an attachment, perhaps, in haste in an attempt to fill the feelings of void following the loss of a relationship. Children were often hurt by the action of a father forming another relationship in a short space of time following the death of their mother. Another anticipatory loss children may face with a new relationship is the loss of a perceived inheritance, or the loss of special sentimental items such as their mother's rings or collection of silver. Divorce and re-partnering affect the energy of the birth family for better and for worse. Children of a first marriage and children of subsequent marriages are frequently wounded by the reading of a will. Unfortunately, money is frequently mistaken for love. Grief takes time, talk, and tears, and is carried on the wheel of life from generation to generation.

The first anniversary was a time when I connected again with the family, to see how they were making adjustments. The specially written computer software alerted the nurse coordinator of anniversary dates. Whatever the circumstances, mindfulness has played a part in keeping my feet on the ground as I supported people following a death. Telephone conversations on occasions of follow up, be they to new or old patients, need to be made mindfully to be effective. When a person is listened to, really listened to, they feel empowered. Being half-listened to by the person on the other end of the phone is not nearly so effective in building a trusting therapeutic relationship. The nurse who was present at the time of death was chosen to make the call, as it is so much harder to connect at a heart level with a person who did not share the moment when the last breath was taken.

One of the most difficult conversations to share in the palliative care context is the conversation on life after death. We are bodies made of condensed light held together by energy which cannot be destroyed and, which after death, leaves the body. One patient who was near death spoke as I stroked her brow and said: "It is all an illusion." She was barely conscious but smiled when she said the words, which provided an answer for her. I struggled to grasp the concept of life as an illusion until I reflected on the iceberg which is a visible form of frozen water. As a chemical compound, a water molecule contains one oxygen and two hydrogen atoms. Water can appear solid when frozen, as a liquid and yet can be an invisible gas. Like the iceberg, the self is partly seen and partly unseen. The unseen part can be likened to the unconscious or dreaming consciousness.

The Dalai Lama and Dr. Elisabeth Kubler-Ross taught that all of our angers and hatred come from fear. Removing fear is the work for those facing end of life and those who support them. Part of living mindfully is to consider our place as a cosmic being made of the same molecules found in the stars. The problem is that most of us can only relate to this time-bound state, and suffering comes when we resist change and seek things to remain as they are.

When not in a mindful state cravings, addictions, and needs of the ego, as described by Eckhart Tolle, the contemporary spiritual teacher, may dominate. These ego needs include thought forms, like expressing strong judgements, being deserving and entitled, as well as having an identification with possessions and status. A mindful state will not act selfishly or get caught up in addictions or the habit of giving stereotyped responses. A person in a mindful state sees things clearly and sees from others' perspective. To have a consistent mindful state in a person's everyday life requires practice. It means to have empathy and to foster, and be receptive to, positive emotions. It does not mean to disengage emotionally or to become indifferent to the situation. To have mindful empathy and non-judgemental awareness can be quite uncomfortable. Empathy differs from sympathy. Sympathy means a simultaneous sharing of feeling with another person. We feel *for* the person. With empathy we project ourselves into the situation as the other person is experiencing it. We attempt to walk mindfully in the other person's shoes.

There are many kinds of meditation. For some it is a prayerful state. For others, it involves calming the mind to achieve a relaxed state. For others, it is seeking the gap between thoughts to achieve an insight or guidance. This guidance may come as intuition or a thought from ego. In Carolyn Myss's book *Entering the Castle*, she writes that it is not difficult to tell the difference, as intuition is relentless and cannot be budged from its position, where ego can be talked into or out of anything. Self-reflection is the essential practice of evaluating your choices against a standard of absolute inner knowing. A sense of contentment seems to be an essential ingredient of meditation. In end-of-life care that may be described as a state of peaceful acceptance. Eckhart Tolle writes that Jesus speaks of the innermost "I Am," the essence identity of every man and woman. Meditation is a pathway to this essence identity.

Florence Nightingale is quoted in *Florence Nightingale - The making of a Radical Theologian*

> What can we know of the Being we call God, but from the manifestation of His nature – His attributes? Look for His thought, His feeling, His purpose; in a word, His spirit within you, without you, behind you, before you. It is indeed omnipresent. Work your true work, and you will find His presence in your self – ie., the presence of those attributes, those qualities, that spirit, which is all we know of God.

The theory of meditation may be easier to understand than the practice. For many years, I would need to be guided by a voice giving me instructions saying to "breathe from the diaphragm. Slowly and deeply breathing in, slowly breathing out…" or "rising and falling" while I focused on abdominal breathing. In 2004, I attended a five-day workshop at the Gawler Foundation in the Yarra Valley, Victoria, to experience the profound natural peace and clarity of deep meditation. It was not difficult to recognise my "monkey mind" when thoughts jumped freely from one idea to another. I tried to image my mind as the clear sun in the sky and thoughts as passing clouds which were blown across the sun by the wind. I can appreciate that discipline and a regular practice are needed by this novice! Another helpful meditation practice is to decide on a word that has meaning and repeat it like a mantra while breathing slowly and deeply. For example, I might use the word 'Yahweh' which is the Hebrew name of God. "Yah" can be spoken softly on the in-breath and "Wey" can be spoken softly on the out-breath

I remember sitting beside a woman who was dying, and wanting to be useful in the vigil, I began to tidy the drawer of her bedside cabinet. There were old and out of date medications, a handkerchief with a hand-crocheted border, a variety of pens and loose slips of paper, as well as a book on meditation by Ainsley Mears. Ainsley Mears, who died in 1986, was an unorthodox Australian psychiatrist who placed meditation at the centre of his therapeutic treatment. This psychiatrist was much ahead of his time and believed that meditation was most effective when pared to its essence, as simple stillness, rather than as a meditative technique.

It did not occur to me that this upper-class lady would have found comfort, and a possible cure for her cancer, in meditation. I feel, without authentic conversations about one's faith and beliefs my supportive care at this precious time is hollow. Yet, I hear time after time, in the traditional palliative care circles, that faith and beliefs are private matters to be respected but not to be shared. The Hospice Chaplain has an important role to play, yet I found it was when I was, as a nurse, attending to daily nursing tasks that a connection between the mundane and the profound could be facilitated. A trusting relationship is the key, and that may be between the person who is dying and a chaplain or with another member of the health team. In the book *Heal Your Mind* by Mona Lisa Schulz with Louise Hay, the advice is to have a health team where the patient is the CEO.

As I wrote those words, I was reminded of the Johari Window, which is a simple and useful tool for illustrating and improving self-awareness and mutual understanding between individuals within a group. This model considers four regions to be explored for mutual understanding.

1. Open area or open self. What the person knows about him/herself and which others also know.
2. Blind area or blind self. What the person doesn't know about him/herself, but which others know
3. Hidden area, hidden self, avoided area or façade. What the person knows about him/herself that others do not know.
4. Unknown area or unknown self. What person doesn't know the about him/herself and which others also do not know.

Also, C. G. Jung's insights into psychological projection may be helpful. In this theory, a perceived personal inferiority or indeed strength is recognised as a perceived moral deficiency or strength to be admired in someone else. So much of the support given to people at the end of their life needs to be given by people who have a degree of awareness of their own conscious and unconscious projections. Florence Nightingale wrote that men and women have souls to unfold and for me, working with people who were dying provided my soul with an opportunity to explore life and death.

I was privileged to have another younger patient who travelled to Melbourne, where Dr. Ainsley Mears practiced, to receive the benefits of his meditation sessions. Unfortunately, I was not well enough informed or appreciative of meditation to connect at a deeper level with her. In this way, I have experienced my patients as my teachers. Dr. Michael Barbato is another Australian doctor who has a special gift for end-of-life care. In his book *Midwifing Death*, he writes about the four domains to midwifing death: They are: Physical Comfort, Healing Environment, Healing Presence, and Spiritual Care. Dr. Barbato writes that death is a profound human experience and needs more than a skilled technician. It needs someone who is prepared to venture into uncharted waters and to silently plumb the hidden passages of their soul. For me, the word "silently" speaks of meditation, and in my assessment portfolio under the heading of spirituality there is a reminder to nurses to do everything with love.

In his book *Life After Death*, Deepak Chopra writes that it doesn't take dying to go beyond thoughts and images. I quote Deepak Chopra: "When someone meditates deeply enough, thoughts disappear and leave only the experience of silence." He writes that consciousness is tied by thousands of threads to old memories, habits, preferences, and relationships, and that we go through life simply making good choices and bad ones. He uses the metaphor of shaping clay with the hand of choice to make who we are today. I strive never to forget the power of praise. Brian Weiss in *Many Lives, Many Masters* concludes: "We all have lessons to learn in the school called Earth. We need to recognise the deceptions and traps of the ego and how to transcend them. We must become aware of the interconnectedness of all living beings, that energy connects us all, and that there is no death, only life."

When I talk to a person at the end of life, my mantra is frequently, "How do you want to be remembered?"

What follows is a ritual I wrote, as a request, for the staff of a nursing home. I call it Remembrance Ritual.

1. Notify all those who are interested of the time and place for the remembrance ritual. An invitation can be computer generated in a personal way.

2. Welcome those who attend with a lighted tea candle in a candle holder, a flower or sprig of rosemary. There may be some appropriate music playing, and some mementos or a photograph of the person in the room.

3. Name the person who has died and invite all present to take a minute of silence to hold that person in their mind's eye and while doing so recall their fondest memories and perhaps what it was in that person that inspired them to also adopt that quality. They may have had a favourite saying or way of looking at life – maybe a smile or a sparkle in their eyes...

4. Take three deliberate breaths in and out, with the out breath longer than the in breath, and thank the person who has died for the way they have touched them.

5. Invite those present to share their memories. This can be done verbally or written on a piece of paper and silently put in a bowl that has been placed on a table or in the middle of the floor. The pieces of paper can be burned in a safe place or released into a flowing stream or sent to an appropriate family member...

6. Following this time invite those present to blow out the candle (if used) and say goodbye to the person - knowing that the ways they have been touched by them will live on in this world by their deeds, their thoughts and their actions.

7. Hold hands and silently make an intention to bring the remembered qualities into one's own life and say 'thank you' to a personal name given to the Divine (God) or the Unseen influences that intuitively guide us.

8. Finish with music and/or a fitting poem or verse of inspiration. There may be refreshments...

9. Take the candle, flower or sprig of rosemary home and resolve to bring the person to mind and the qualities that will live on in you for a period of three or more days.

10. Have the computer record the date of death and on the first Anniversary send a card or make phone contact.

CHAPTER 10

The Journey into Soul Deepens

The unconscious may be understood in terms of the Myers-Briggs Typology.

This can happen by reflecting on our least preferred way of living in the world (the Inferior Function). As a palliative care nurse, I often observed the Inferior Function when the effects of medication or lack of energy made it difficult for the patient to keep a lid on suppressed emotion. The expression of these emotions can be very hurtful to those at the bedside, and needed explanation and normalisation. The rituals of confession and forgiveness in some form have a place in preparing for death. These rituals can be performed by a priest or minister and have a religious context or be as simple as a loving touch and a nod of understanding by whoever is present. It is the intention that matters. I have experienced a gentleman or gentlewoman well versed in politeness and the longtime practice of manners, as death approaches, express anger, resentment, guilt, and regret. Enormous sensitivity and understanding is required by those who support souls at this time of life. Jung taught the importance of having an understanding of the psychological concept of projection.

I appreciated having this awareness. I could see that there was a danger among carers of projecting their own death anxiety or unresolved issues onto the person receiving care. Simply, we tend to see in the other that which we do not recognize in ourselves. My personal experience was evident when I unconsciously related to patients who had the potential for a bedsore. My father had died with a bedsore, and I was projecting feelings for my father onto the patients whose skin was damaged from pressure. Self-awareness and insights into personality are of paramount importance for those who seek to work in a caring role. We cannot give away what we do not have by way of consciousness ourselves. Another way of saying this is that we can only take people as far as we have travelled along the road of understanding the purpose and meaning of life. Palliative care, to be effective, is so much more than administering medications. It is about the invisible but important task of listening to the needs of the patient's soul.

In 2015, I visited an Ashram in Southern India, with Andrew Harvey as my guide. Again, the metaphor of the tree was used to describe our connectedness with the Source of all life via the roots. With the unconscious mind, we all tap into synchronicity, déjà vu, and statements such as: "I was just thinking of you (when the phone rang)" or on waking from a dream state finding that the solution to a problem becomes clear. I have gained insights from making a vision board from cut-out pictures from everyday life as a way of getting clear on what is a perceived need, want, or value. The intention may be to attract representations of the chosen images and words into the life. Colouring mandalas is another practice gaining attention. Carol Omer, the author of *The Big Girls' Little Coloring Book*, writes: "*Mandala* is a Sanskrit word for 'circle,' and in the twenty-first century world of concrete, technology, and complexities, returning to the circle that mirrors the womb of creation provides a time for rest, reflection, relaxation, and fun!"

In drawing or colouring in these circular patterns and symbols a support for meditation and connecting with one's inner life can be found.

Esoteric philosophy and the ancient Hindu spiritual tradition refer to a state of consciousness as the Akashic Field, where all thoughts and actions are stored. Jean Houston calls it 'the ground of being' where all patterns exist and seeds can be planted with the intention of manifestation. She says that we can become conduits for sacred energy. Once this energy is breathed in it can be breathed out and directed to those in need. This can be thought of as another form of prayer. Thomas Hubl refers to the Akashic Field as 'the book of life' or The Book. Others, like Ervin Laszlo, who is a member of both the International Academy of Science, World Academy of Arts and Science, and the International Academy of Philosophy, link the world of science with spiritual traditions. His work in recent years has centred on the formulation and development of the "Akasha Paradigm," a new conception of cosmos, life and consciousness emerging at the forefront of the contemporary sciences.

As I have grown older, I felt the need to delve deeper into the larger and more spiritual questions of life. I read books about the psychic information provided by Edgar Cayce, who as a medical intuitive, described timeless consciousness to inspire a larger world view and a holistic approach to healing. With this broadening of my mental horizon I have explored other techniques such as Shamanic drumming and self-hypnosis to discourage thoughts and doubts from clouding this source of wisdom and guidance. The turtle is my Shamanic power animal. It is a symbol for long life, and I'm amazed at how many people from different backgrounds give me different art forms of the turtle.

Caroline Myss helped me to understand the world of archetypes. She writes that archetypes have been around since the time of Plato. C. G. Jung described archetypes as universal, archaic patterns and images that derive from the collective unconscious and are the psychic counterparts of instinct. In order to determine which archetypes are most active in one's psyche, Myss devised a unique set of cards.

She, like Jung, suggests that most archetypes are psychological or energy patterns and include: Mother, Child, Victim, Healer, Queen, King, Servant, Bully, Computer Geek, Prostitute, and Saboteur. This work helped me to remove yet more snow. For example, the Prostitute archetype helped me to realize when I am "selling" a principle or belief for the sake of peace or laziness. An understanding of the Mother archetype also gave me an appreciation of the Divine Feminine whose principles are nurturing, love and understanding, insight and intuition, creativity, forgiveness and healing. The Divine Feminine incorporates several archetypes for the different periods in one's life, and is in all mystical traditions. I know, and people sense, when my Duchess archetype walks into a room.

However, archetypes also have shadows, and Myss describes the shadow of the Mother archetype 'is' as a devouring, abusive, and abandoning mother. It seems that there are so many pathways to follow in my endeavour to know myself. Sister Margaret Cain, who was a wise and visionary member of the Dominican Order, gave me a sacred mantra to guide my life: "Life has meaning when you give yourself meaning."

Several trips to Greece with Jean Houston, the American author who encourages people to live from their supreme destiny, introduced me to the Golden Age of Greece and insights from the myths of the Ancient Greek gods and goddesses such as Athena, Hera, Persephone, Athena, Apollo, Aphrodite, Hermes, and Artemis. I particularly related to Persephone, the goddess who was queen of the underworld, and the bride of Hades. She was abducted by Hades, and I can relate to being abducted or called to my work with people who are dying. Persephone worked as a guide for humans to gain full knowledge of themselves, including the dark places of their personality. It is said that Persephone had knowledge of the end and the beginning of life.

With beginnings and endings, or births and deaths, in mind, I explored the writing of Alice Baily whose works, written between 1919 and 1949, describe a wide-ranging system of esoteric thought, covering such topics as how spirituality relates to the solar system, meditation, healing, spiritual psychology, the destiny of nations, and prescriptions for society in general. She described the majority of her work as having been telepathically dictated to her by a Master of Wisdom, referred to only as "the Tibetan." Her writings were somewhat similar to those of Madame Blavatsky, who is the founder of the Theosophical Society, and are among the teachings often referred to as "Ageless Wisdom." All this is very profound, and there are times that I appreciate the wisdom of the Tao, a spiritual, philosophical, and religious tradition of Chinese origin, which means Way or Path. The Tao states that "the Tao that can be known is not the Tao." Certainly, the World Wide Web and smart phones produce magic that I can use but not understand. It is no wonder that the Mind of God cannot be known.

Very early in my nurse practice, I had computer software programs specially written for the patient and staff records, and the activities connected to payroll and other employer responsibilities. It seemed that if I had to do this work myself, it had to be done in the most proficient manner with regards to time and accuracy. I wanted my nurse practice specialising in palliative care for the private sector to be a model demonstrating how a nurse could give personalised care as well as attend to the administrative responsibilities of her own business. I built my practice on word of mouth referrals, and employed palliative care assistants on a casual basis to maintain flexibility. The motto was, "The Patient First Always" and by offering a twenty-four-hour helpline, patients felt more empowered to self-manage. It was in my personality to challenge the way people were cared for at the end of their life. My creative imagination sought to extend the profession of nursing to include a model of self-employed case coordination. It is common for other allied health professionals such as physiotherapists, dieticians, and speech therapists to offer a private practice, so why not a nurse?

Most spiritual traditions teach that we are so much more than our personality and body image, although these attributes contribute to the way we live in the world. Today, I live alone, except when children or grandchildren come to stay. This gives me plenty of time for inward-looking activities. Computer card games, Sudoku, and "sticking to the facts" reflections and writing exercise my thinking function, while meditation requires a gap between thoughts. In a workshop conducted by William Meader, who is formally trained in Esoteric Philosophy, I learned more about my soul's journey and how, in the language of Esoteric Philosophy, my personality needs to fuse with my soul or causal body to become my Higher or True Self. In this line of exploration, the personality is made up of thinking, emotional, and physical "bodies." Esoteric Astrology has become a further tool to increase self-awareness, and assists in a cosmic view point. The word "shadow", which I was familiar with from a Jungian perspective, was also used by William Meader to demonstrate the distortions of spiritual truth.

Another tool for self-awareness, which I experienced many times, is the Enneagram. The Enneagram is a powerful approach to understanding the psychology, emotions and behavior of ourselves and others. It has its origins in ancient wisdom traditions and is designed to assist a person to pay attention to their primary drives, passions, and compulsions. On a circular diagram there are nine numbers, which are divided into three centres. One group of three numbers represents a heart centre, another group of three numbers represents a head centre and a third represents the gut centre. This subtle and complex nine pointed tool gave me the awareness that my "boss" or "challenger" self in the eight gut centre would benefit from moving to the "two" in the heart centre and working to assist the community at large. This meant that I would be more open and reveal my vulnerability, and by so doing become more concerned for others and more loving. When, as an "eight", I move to the positive side of the "five" head centre I see things from a more objective point of view and think more before acting. I have at times moved to the negative side of the "five" head centre and felt defeated, thinking that everything I wanted to achieve was too difficult, and become depressed.

It has also been insightful to contemplate the different functions of the brain. For example, intuition is a function of the right side of the brain. I know that I am very intuitive and less inclined to value science and logic. Albert Einstein wrote that the intuitive mind is a sacred gift, and the rational mind is a faithful servant. Florence Nightingale seemed to be gifted with both the left and right functions of the brain. Emeritus Professor Ian Maddocks, AM, who is an eminent palliative care specialist and a passionate advocate for world peace, was a frequent presenter in NurseLink's education programs. The following is from a slide presentation to NurseLink Foundation in 2011:

The brain is a single organ. We all have both left and right hemispheres: We need them both, and must value them both, seeking the best ways to have them work as one.

We need clarity and precision, plus intuition and faith
We need science and need the arts
We need facts and we need metaphor
We need distance and engagement
We need objectivity and love.

He spoke of the need to be in awe of the many unknowns we face and to know our patients and ourselves as spiritual beings. The education programs I ran revealed participants often preferred left-brain topics rather than right-brain topics, which could be interpreted as airy-fairy. Yet it is the world behind the eyes that needs exploring in order to understand soul needs.

Traditional religions have played a large part in my search for Truth. My parents were both very active in the Methodist church. I grew to love the hymns and my mother's playing of the church organ. Yet in many ways, I was uncomfortable with my parent's goodness. Obviously, my inquiring "small self" needed to do its own soul searching. At school and during my training to become a registered nurse, I occasionally attended an Anglican church. In my early twenties, I married a man who was a Roman Catholic and I adopted this religion for many years. Following my divorce, I spent time in East and West Malaysia and developed an interest in Eastern Philosophies.

Today, I call myself an agnostic Buddhist–Catholic with a Methodist upbringing and a person who says Hindu mantras and meditates. I gain great faith by studying the Sufi mystics and agree with Rumi that there are many lamps (as in religions and paths) but only one light. I am interested in the teachings on chakras from Hindu and Taoist traditions. I like to gain wisdom and insights from meditation. I seek to know myself—the conscious and unconscious parts (including the dream world). I view God as a cosmic force likened to a giant computer, and all life as work stations connected to the computer or mind of God as co-creators of all that is, if we make choices with that intention. I believe in reincarnation and see my soul travelling through multiple lifetimes. Each lifetime my soul takes on a new personality in order to learn lessons that will move my personality (ego) from imperfect to perfect. I understand my personality to be made up of a mental body, an emotional body and a physical body. I understand that, as energy forms, we evolve and become more consciousness of the underlying fact that we are all connected to the One Consciousness, which many call God.

Early in my career, Sogyal Rinpoche's *The Tibetan Book of Living and Dying* guided me in deep understanding of the needs of the dying person. Decades later, and perhaps by fate, I was to meet an editor of that book, Andrew Harvey, on my travels to Southern India. Primarily, I learned that I needed to conquer my own fear of death and to pay particular attention to resolving any unfinished business the person who is dying may have as early as possible. In short, I needed to be a trusted, non-judgemental loving, kind and calm listener who is aware of the psychological states of projection and transference as well as personal karma.

I believe that the way in which we live our lives and our state of mind at death directly influence the soul's journey. The aim of a person who seeks to know their spiritual path and trusts in a perception of being a co-creator with the Universe will have no fear or regrets at the time of death. Essential to Buddhism is a belief in karma and reincarnation. Sogyal Rinpoche writes that ego, or the small self, is defined as incessant attempts to grasp a delusory notion of "I" and "mine" and all the concepts, ideas, desires, and activity that will sustain that false construction. Pain and suffering come with attachment and aversion. I needed to be aware of what was being clung to unrealistically, and what was being avoided and not being addressed? Buddhism introduced me to "Om mani padme hum," which is the mantra of the Buddha of compassion. This mantra is said to purify each of the negative emotions that are the cause of rebirth. I have a small white statue of Kwan Yin, who is the goddess of compassion, in my home and love her as well as call on her to protect my children and grandchildren. In striving to understand the Divine Feminine energy, I relate to the goddess Tara in her many forms. Spiritual teacher Mirabai Starr describes her:

> Green Tara represents Mother Earth and gives comfort, protection and interconnectedness such as the root system which holds us together.

> White Tara represents maternal compassion, healing and reconciliation – call on her when there is disharmony.

> Red Tara represents discriminating awareness – cuts through illusion and lays the truth bare. She is discerning and wise.

> Blue Tara represents the wild sensual one (like the Hindu goddess Kali) uncontained and untamed – she will do anything to set us free.

Tara lives inside me - as does Mother Mary and Kwan Yin - and are examples of Divine Feminine energy.

Mantras are repetitions used in meditation. I seem to have favourites from many traditions to use in my walks and quiet times. I note Rumi's wise words: "Why are you knocking at every other door? Go, knock at the door of your own heart."

My understanding is that thoughts at the time of death are conveyed clairvoyantly and I have often reminded families of the power of thought and the need for love and right intention at the bedside of a person who is dying. When my grandchildren ask about my religion I reply as did the Sufi mystic Ibn Arabi: "I follow the religion of love."

> Information lacks the power of transformation, whereas "knowledge" is the carrier of sacred and eternal truths that awaken your psyche and soul or, more accurately, wake you up to what you were born already knowing.
> —Carolyn Myss

I would like to convey that life is a preparation for death and that the soul is the part of us that does not die. It carries with it the experiences of the personality, which is made up of the emotional body with all its joys and sorrows, the mental body with all its clarity and confusion, and the physical body which is a reflection of inner and outer health. I wish to convey the importance of understanding that all is energy, which cannot be destroyed. At death, the energy leaves the body and carries soul particles of experiences with it into future lifetimes. The highest vibration of energy is love, and a good death is dependent on the quality of the love vibration and the degree of detachment the personality or ego has from all things worldly.

Karma, which is the result of choices, affects every aspect of the personality. There are different levels of consciousness which need to be understood in this lifetime, as well as different levels of consciousness in the afterlife. Souls travel from lifetime to lifetime and have the choice of co-creating with the One Consciousness, which is often referred to as God or a "super computer" to which we are connected.

I wish to convey that the dream state is the interface between this world and the next, and the value of meditation in accessing what C. G. Jung called the collective unconscious for guidance and connection at a deep level. I wish to convey the importance of relationship: with self, with others, and with God. Life is for learning and it is never too late to start a new profession or to follow a calling. I wish to convey the benefits of not outsourcing our graduation from this earthly plane entirely to the medical profession, even if they practice with an integrative approach to well-being. Finally, I wish to convey that those souls who leave behind their earthly bodies will be met with understanding. Elisabeth Kubler-Ross called this state of transition as having all knowledge.

CHAPTER 11

Reflecting on Chakra Energy

The traditional Hindu system of belief encompasses energy centres known as chakras, which serve to accumulate, assimilate, and transmit psychological, physical, and spiritual energies.

This personal sharing is an attempt to listen to guidance from my soul in the knowledge that I have a body but that I am more than my body. My soul is striving to bring my personality, which is made up of a physical body, an emotional body and a mental body, into alignment with my Higher Self (Divine Spark) or soul. To move forward in this process, I have felt the need to shed the weight of the past, which has the potential to slow my soul's effort to become future orientated. This is like pulling up the anchor of my small boat on the river of life. In my effort to grow and be free from the burden of the past with its habitual thinking and emotional patterns, I have used my small knowledge of the chakras as a template for reflection. Parts of the body are associated with the chakra energy system and give a clue as to what area of my life I need to heal.

THE FIRST CHAKRA IS THE BASE CHAKRA.

This chakra is found at the base of the spine and is the foundation of emotional and mental health, and, as such, this chakra required much work on my part. It is the connection to family beliefs and customs, and supports the foundations of identity and belonging in a group or tribe. It is about safety and security and the ability to provide for life's necessities and to feel at home in the world. It is about the ability to determine values and to sense one's purpose in life. In this space, I feel the influence of my ancestors, parents, children, school, and other friends and professional peers. What comes through strongly is the need to be true to myself and not to trade what for me, is truth for the sake of popularity or merely being agreeable. I like to be honest in all dealings. "Honesty is the best policy," I have often said to my children and grandchildren. I feel blessed to have grown up in a country environment and to have had loving parents who gave me the freedom to be who I was meant to be. Grandparents also passed on their genetic DNA in many ways. Different tribes gave me different lessons to learn.

I have early memories of a self-sufficient maternal grandparents' home. My aunt made butter from milk which came straight from the household cow. Fruit and vegetables were grown with pride. Needle work was encouraged for idle hands. The driveway to this home was covered with gravel and, as a child, I would search for the smallest stones so that I could play How Many Eggs in my Basket? In this game each player would have ten small stones and, with hands hidden behind their back, would place a number of stones (not more than five) in a closed fist and ask the question: "How many eggs in my basket?" If the opponent guessed correctly they earned the stones, but would have to make up the difference from their supply and give to the other if they guessed incorrectly.

I would be fascinated looking for small, cone-shaped holes in the garden soil, where an insect had burrowed down. These were such simple pleasures, but demonstrated being one with nature and the use one's imagination for pleasure. Such was my family tribe. This experience was followed by my connections with my boarding school tribe and forming lasting friendships under the leadership of an extraordinary headmistress.

With my marriage I left my family tribe to enter into, and learn from, new tribes. My family tribe was formed on the Protestant religion and the manners of an English gentleman. The new tribe of my husband's family was Catholic with an Irish heritage. Like life in my former tribes, I questioned the rules. One in particular was birth control. Other tribes were entered into and were formed with professional friends and our children's school communities. Following our divorce, friends from this tribe largely left me out in the cold. This is so often witnessed in cases where the reputation of the firm, church, or school is more valued than that of the individual. My husband and I were members of the same golf club. When news of our divorce reached the club, I remember going into the dining room after a game. The atmosphere was heavy with silent questioning and disapproval. I will always remember the kindness of one member who invited me to lunch with her. Later, I learned that this member had already had her lunch. That is what it means to be empathic.

When I returned to nursing and was working part-time in a Catholic hospice, my creative mind wanted to change the way patients were nursed and records were kept. I was an early admirer of the computer and could see many uses for it in the hospice setting. I would go home, and on my home computer, write creative care plans which I now know to be considerate of the whole person. I remember travelling to a Hospice Conference in Montreal, Canada, and returning with all sorts of ideas for hospice care. They were largely rejected. Looking back, I can see that change was very threatening to the hospice at that time, but I didn't stop writing copious suggestions to the nuns, who were a tribe I admired.

I began a Foundation to enable them to raise much needed funds, and put heart and soul into the work. It was not to be my tribe for long. I was being pushed out of that tribe to go it alone in a private nurse practice. I remember being asked by one of the nuns what was the matter with me? I replied that I was used to being boss, and received the answer that I was not going to be! I was presented with the choice of staying in an environment without appreciation or taking control of my own life. I remember one kindly nun likening my situation to walking through mud wearing gum boots. In 1987, I formed a company called Private Palliative Care Services Pty Ltd. My social friends thought hospice was a charity for other people. I wanted to demonstrate that it was for everyone who appreciated having their needs and ways of living cared for in a private model which put them in charge. Dr Elisabeth Kubler-Ross had a tribe of followers, and I was an admiring member of that tribe.

I questioned the values and merits of all the tribes which played a part in my life. I did note, however, that when I left a tribe, the tribe closed ranks behind me. This was a way soul led my life, pushing me forward as one door after another closed. I needed to stand on my own and go it alone on so many fronts. As with the migrating birds, so surely with us, there is a voice within, if only we would listen to it. The inner voice tells us, so certainly, when to go forth into the unknown. It may not be a comfortable place or an easy life, but it is important to live an authentic life. Tribal influences resulted in wisdom or woe. From my tribes, I see the common thread of all religions to be loving and compassionate. I am not afraid to speak my truth and to seek mentors in the area of spiritual growth. The first chakra is associated with physical energy in the lower back, colon, legs, and feet. I have had long periods with lower back pain and, difficult to diagnose, swelling in my legs and feet.

Healing has come with a new tribe called Soul Talks. Like Florence Nightingale, I know God to be a "presence higher than human" and to be a divine intelligence that creates, sustains, and organizes the universe to which we have an inner connection, and that heaven is neither a place nor a time. Today my tribe is Soul Talks. This charity seeks to encourage the pursuit of mental and emotional health by offering a platform and support for health practitioners who practice integrative health.

THE SECOND CHAKRA IS THE SEXUAL CHAKRA.

This chakra is the centre of personal power, creativity, sexuality, physical survival, and one-to-one relationships. It is found in the lower abdomen of the body.

My second son, when I began my nurse practice, sent me a Mother's Day card. It depicted a woman running through a park with the caption: "After motherhood everything is a breeze!" How nearly true! Those years of three children under three and four children when the eldest was just five were tough indeed. My first child was born in London, England. My daughter was born in Rochester, New York. My two youngest children were born in Adelaide, South Australia, where we had no family members to offer practical support. My salvation came in the form of La-la who was a delightful Danish lady who had a longing for grandchildren. She became my children's adopted grandmother and provided a valuable and supportive relationship.

This wonderful woman was forever patient and a wonderful cook. She regularly filled the cookie tins, which were large Milo tins. She made chicken liver paté and Danish open hors d'oeuvres as well as Danish pastries. We all loved her! I digress to tell you about her death. Her husband had died some years prior and when La-la found herself a double amputee from diabetes she insisted on going home to her little cottage, which she had converted to make for easy living. She insisted on living alone and said, after a trial of respite in a nursing home, that she would lose her mind if she stayed there. I feel I would too, and trust that is not a part of my destiny. I was proud to learn that my youngest son, as a sixteen year old, had slept two nights with her to keep her company when she first came home from being in care.

There were times when La-la needed care from the nurses I employed in my practice, but she mostly managed with her lowered bench tops, chairs, and bed, which she could slide to from her wheelchair. She had always told her two sons that when she died, they were to call Mrs. Nugent. It was almost as if she had knowledge and guidance from the other side. She certainly was free from fear. One night, around 7 p.m., when I was in the office attending to paperwork, I had a phone call from a daughter-in-law asking me to come, as they had found La-la on the floor. When I arrived, it was evident that she had died in a peaceful way and after the formalities of calling a doctor we gently put her into her bed, washed and dressed her. It was an unbelievably special time and a way I could say thank you for all the love and care she had given to our family. At that time, I was regularly away in Brisbane where I had a second practice. Yet she chose to die at such a convenient time for me and her family. Who decides the moment of death?

This chakra is about relationships. Relationships need to be considered on three fronts. One relationship is with oneself. Another is with others and a third is with one's God. After living alone for twenty-five years, I can understand how an intimate relationship with a partner can be a distraction from a way of life, which is totally consumed with a relationship with one's soul or Higher Self. Perhaps I have experienced a withdrawal to a monastery in a past life? There were times when I became aware that feelings with the tendency to project onto another can also be claimed by my *animus* and be fulfilled in ways that do not need to be projected onto another human. The union of the male and female aspects of the self can be part of the individuation process or becoming conscious of the whole self that Jung wrote about.

In my work, I often encountered couples from Eastern religions who lived in a marriage chosen by others, growing in love rather than falling in love. While the ending of my marriage was a difficult time for me, I was forced to grow in so many ways. I believe that each partner in a marriage needs to fulfill their life as an individual soul and live together with mutual respect. However, I grew to realise that it is better to save a soul than to save a marriage. At the time of my divorce my children were young adults and had been supported as best we, as parents, knew how. I wonder about past life influences and agreements and the concept of fate and destiny. Sometimes, I question the benefits of having no choice. This is the case when people are dying. At that time, I would say, so often, that love is letting go. While the marriage relationship has gone, we unite to celebrate family occasions like weddings and Christmas.

My nurse practice was built on relationship, and sharing that profound deep experience inspired me to keep going for three decades. In many ways it became my identity, and gave me a false sense of self. One man used to say, "It is Joy who cometh in the morning." I was never good at night duty, but would sleep with the phone by my bed in support of the palliative care assistant who was spending the hours by the bedside in that supportive role of being my eyes and hands. My nursing was an example of my creative expression. Sexuality was expressed as Sacred Sexuality; however, I did flirt a little with patients who were dying or over ninety! This chakra leads to physical health for the reproductive organs, bladder, kidney, and the endocrine gland. I had difficulty becoming pregnant with our first child and needed a hysterectomy at the age of forty. Kidney function is variable and fluid retention is on-going.

THE THIRD CHAKRA IS THE SOLAR PLEXUS CHAKRA.

This chakra is about self-esteem, personality, boundaries and a sense of self, which is not related to the tribe of the first chakra or the power and relationship struggles of the second chakra. It is about living an authentic life without the masks and manners society may demand. It is recognising the different levels of consciousness and exploring the hidden self or what Jung referred to as the shadow. It is about having the self-confidence to handle any situation without seeking someone's approval. It is about confidence and perseverance in one's life task or mission. Creating my private nurse practice was a lonely time, and there were times when I felt the need for approval from the mainstream palliative care organisations who seemed to be secure in their multidisciplinary teams. Being appreciated by my friends and colleagues in the Sandakan Hospice in East Malaysia fulfilled a need to be useful and appreciated. My work was better known there than it was in my home town of Adelaide. I loved being greeted with orchids and smiling faces when I stepped off the plane.

For many years after my divorce, I was a member of the National Speakers Association. In hindsight, this organisation gave me much by way of self-esteem. I attended various workshops and conferences. In particular, I remember one workshop where we were not allowed to tell other participants our names or background—rather we communicated using intuition. That organisation assisted me greatly, although when we met for our monthly meeting and people would be sharing their topics, I noticed the clearing of space around me when I used say that my topic was "death and dying!"

In my public speaking, I have never tried to perform but rather to trust to inner wisdom and strive to be "in the moment" and to follow what comes up by way of thoughts and memories. I think the expression is 'being in the zone.' I was not one to throw people in the audience sweeties as an attention grabber. Having said that, I do like to use a PowerPoint Presentation to keep me focused. I need to see the written word as well as hear it. I believe that my Diploma in Clinical Hypnosis obtained at the age of seventy-five gave me pointers as to how my message could be remembered. Even before I added this skill to my education, people would come up to me and say that they attended one of my courses in palliative long after the event. I believe this is soul speaking to soul.

I have always used stories to illustrate the theory, and aimed to be my authentic self in the sharing of information. I saw myself as an entrepreneur, and the literature suggests that entrepreneurs need to be supported. They get shot at! I rarely felt supported and was indeed shot at. After all, I was only a nurse with a basic hospital-based apprenticeship-style qualification. I have always believed in self-directed learning, and if I felt that I needed to be updated in an area, I would do just that.

When I began my private nurse practice, I needed to create all the forms and, most importantly, an Assessment Portfolio. Again, I was to be the rebel; this time against the jargon used by nurses to make them feel more professional. I wrote nursing diagnosis in lay language and encouraged people to work out their own care plans. For example, the heading Activities and Rest was followed by 'a' why it was being considered and offered suggestions that may be helpful. I could not see the sense in writing a care plan unless it was what the patient wanted, and was one that they owned. This education encouraged self-responsibility and the involvement of family. This area in my life was never easy. The third chakra is experienced as physical energy in the adrenals, pancreas, digestive system, liver, and gall bladder. No wonder my gall bladder needed to be removed when it was found to be full of dice-shaped stones!

For many years I played the game of golf, and this game was perfect discipline for me. I had lesson after lesson and practiced enough to have an enjoyable game at a B grade level. I loved to hit the long ball, which, all too often, would land in a bunker. I used to call golf "the game of life", for there were so many lessons requiring skill and luck. During my years playing golf, I lost much useless fear, and certainly gained much in confidence as well as physical exercise and concentration. I needed to know myself. In this endeavour, I learned much from the MBTI. I recommend this well-researched, introspective, self-reporting questionnaire inventory for learning one's preferred way of living in the world and how to understand and appreciate differences among other people. I also valued the Enneagram, a powerful approach to understanding the psychology, emotions, and behaviour of ourselves and others. It describes the gifts and the challenges of each personality style and has its origins in ancient wisdom traditions.

My inner knowing tells me that my purpose in this lifetime is to advocate for change in the way elderly people are cared for in nursing homes. To my mind, rules and regulations tied to funding could be replaced with a more soulful lifestyle - a community of genuine care. Florence Nightingale's advice to nurses in Tasmania was "To be a good nurse you need to be a good person." She also wrote on ways to unify science and spirituality to bring order, meaning and purpose to human life. Her writings gave my life a purpose.

THE FOURTH CHAKRA IS THE HEART CHAKRA.

Caroline Myss describes this centre as the powerhouse of the human energy system. It is about forgiveness of self and others and the ability to heal self and others. It connects body and soul in the medium of love. We all need to give love and receive it. I repeat the wisdom of spiritual leader Ram Dass to my grandchildren, and say that all we have to do in life is to love everyone and to tell the truth.

Most of us will remember the pain of our first romantic love and the hurt when school friends were mean and cruel. There are also the times when parents don't understand and cause a young one to go behind their backs on decisions. I frequently lost connection with my artistic and musical mother, who suffered from depression, and I found comfort in the visualisation of seeing my mother as a child and, together, dancing in the space of my heart. As a nurse, I would try to see other professionals, who thought my work should be stopped, receiving loving beams of light. This was not easy! I took comfort in the fact that if I was being criticised I must be doing something worthwhile.

Memories of my first love are both painful and pleasurable. While I completed my nursing qualifications, the first love of my life was studying in the US. After graduation, I worked in St. Joseph's Hospital, Toronto, while waiting to be admitted to a midwifery course in Edinburgh, Scotland. Before traveling to Scotland I visited my heart connection for a week of sailing on the Sacramento River in California. Imagine the thrill of the wind, the sounds of the water and birds, and a beautiful blissful connectedness. We did become formally engaged when I was in London and his sister, who was living in England, was the bearer of a diamond ring from a New York jeweller. I was stunned and grieved when I received a "Dear John" letter and that beautiful first romance ended.

I took comfort in the saying that it is better to have loved and lost than never to have loved at all. It was embarrassing telling family and friends that the engagement period had ended, but I do not recall any anger or jealousy. I didn't know, at that stage of my life, about grief as I do now. I did know that there was chemistry between two people. I remember a male student of some facility in Edinburgh driving me to the Lake District in England and suggesting more than friendship, but it seemed that loyalty to one person at a time was the order of the day for me.

At the time of my divorce, I was reading *The Road Less Travelled* by M. Scott Peck, the American psychiatrist. In his writing, he makes the point that if one of a couple comes to him for personal growth and the desire to live more deeply and the other does not, they invariably separate. It was an inquiring but lonely time for me, as discussions on a soul level were not welcomed by my husband.

I threw myself into my professional life and resigned from the golf club and another prestigious Adelaide women's club. I travelled to palliative care conferences in India, Singapore, the UK, Canada and Malaysia, and constantly pursued self-knowledge and awareness. I conducted courses for nurses and carers in Adelaide, South Australia country, and in Queensland and yet the feeling persisted that I needed to do more. In 2005, I self-published six books in a series: *A passion for Caring.*

Book 1 *A Blueprint for Holistic Care*
Book 2 *Creative Supportive Care*
Book 3 *Holistic Experiences of Loss and Grief*
Book 4 *Soul Talk and Complementary Therapies*
Book 5 *Applying Holistic Skills in Dementia Care*
Book 6 *Creative Self Development*

Nature is a great healer and the inner message I received was "God removes from your life that which is no longer useful." At a deep level, I know that if we get death right we get life right. Emotional pain or heart pain follows loss. This loss may be loss of reputation, job, possessions, status, body image and so much more. It will happen and it is how a person deals with loss that shapes attitude, character, and connectedness to something greater than our small self.

People I have loved are many. It has been my gift to those in my care. There are also things I have loved. My first real experience of love and loss came on my fifth birthday. My parents had organised a birthday call on the radio for me. The radio voice told me where to find a big box. In the box was a doll as big as a real baby. I had never seen anything so beautiful, and made a bed for the doll in the box. I still remember the joy. However, it was to be short-lived for when I tried to lift the box and doll from the couch, the doll came tumbling out and dropped to the floor, and the head smashed into many pieces. I was inconsolable for weeks, and although the head was repaired, it was never the doll I fell in love with. A new head was eventually obtained and the lesson was that a replacement, however near the original, is not the same.

This is a lesson for parents of children who experience the death of a pet. It is wrong to think that another pet can be the solution without a period of grief for the original pet. Grief is so much more than theory that resides in the head; it is primarily a function of the heart chakra. In my book *My Way: One Nurses Passion for End of Life,* I tell the story of my three-year-old self being wounded when my father drowns my mummy cat's kittens. The mummy cat cried and searched for them in a way that broke my little heart. Perhaps these early lessons of heartbreak led me to do my life's work as a palliative care nurse.

The energy of the heart chakra is very helpful when two people connect in this space. Sharing emotional pain is quite bonding. The heart chakra vibrates with compassion and effects the vibrations of the other person's energy. The archetype of the wounded healer is well recognised. I am also aware of psychological projection when people defend themselves against their own unconscious impulses or qualities (both positive and negative) by denying their existence in themselves while seeing them in others.

Unconscious feelings are also transferred onto another. When feelings are returned there is an experience of counter transference. I remember a participant in one of my presentations saying that I reminded her of her aunt and shared those feelings, positive and negative! These insights form the foundation for a different way of experiencing oneself and relating to others. Mother Teresa, who worked with the poor and dying in India, gave an example of transference when she said, "I see my beloved (Jesus) in everyone and I'm so in love with my beloved that I can't do enough for my beloved and my beloved can't do enough for me."

The Greeks had four names for love:

> *Agape* referred to a kind of love that one associates with brotherly love, good will, benevolence and the unconditional love of God for his children, as well as the love for all things Godly.

> *Eros* relates to passionate love of a sexual or intimate nature. From Plato we learn about love that is an appreciation of the beauty within that person. So Platonic love is love without physical attraction.

Philia means affectionate regard, friendship and a dispassionate virtuous love showing loyalty to friends and family. It was developed by Aristotle and requires virtue, equality and familiarity.

Storge may be described as natural empathy, like that felt by parents for offspring and family members in general. It is also known to express mere acceptance or putting up with situations.

The word forgiveness looms large in the care and support given to those who are dying. I have listened to stories of theft, deceit, betrayal, and remorse. Elderly people still remember a small injustice that took place many years ago.

The following are some thoughts and guiding principles that were food for my soul when I reflect on the emotional pain of loss and grief.

The pain of grief is just as much a part of life as the joy of love; it is perhaps the price we pay for love, the cost of commitment. To ignore this fact, or to pretend that it is not so is to put on emotional blinkers which leave us unprepared for the losses that will inevitably occur in our lives and unprepared to help others cope with the losses in theirs (Dr Colin Murray Parkes).

There is no end point to grief - an unexpected reminder of a past loss may trigger more grief. The pain of yearning may diminish with time; talk and tears and age, sex, circumstances, and world philosophy all affect the process, and each story is particular to the individual. A blockage in heart energy affects heart and lung function as well as the upper back and shoulders. When I returned from 'in' Malaysia for three months, I had tests to establish the health of my heart. I had gone to Ipoh following my divorce and at the invitation of a local oncologist. The intention was to assist this oncologist in setting up a private hospice. There followed much heartache, and many difficulties were put in the way of making this a successful venture. That period in my life was full of sorrow and strain.

We need silence to be able to touch souls. The essential thing is not what we say, but what God says to us and through us. All our words will be useless unless they come from within (Mother Teresa).

THE FIFTH CHAKRA IS THE THROAT CHAKRA.

This energy centre is about communication, strengthening will and learning resilience. It is also about speaking one's truth.

Perhaps one of my most interesting throat experiences occurred at a Leadership and Spirituality conference held on the Australian Gold Coast. I had been asked to be a speaker about my work as a private palliative care nurse. I had also just completed a course in neuro-linguistic programming and remember asking the audience to close their eyes and to see in their left hand a situation they would like to change and then to focus on the solution the right hand was offering. I recalled a situation that I needed to change as a hot potato in my left hand. I needed to bounce the hot potato frequently in order not to burn my hand. Then I saw in my mind's eye the desired result in my right hand as a pink marshmallow! I was being told to look at the situation in a calm soft manner rather than a jumpy angry manner. Symbols and metaphors are an effective way of communicating what is sometimes beyond words.

As I walked out of one of the sessions, I was invited to look into a mirror and to note what I saw. All I could see was my throat. That evening I had a raging sore throat. The throat chakra was demanding attention. It also demanded my attention just after my marriage ended. A neurosurgeon was to operate on the vertebrae in my neck to relieve a pinched nerve that was causing pain in my left arm. A disc was removed and C6 and C7 vertebrae were fused with a circle of bone taken from a pig. The first attempt at relieving the neuropathic pain in my left arm failed, and more surgery was needed to remove a spur that was pinching the nerve. My throat chakra was being well and truly strengthened for what lay ahead of me. From the security of marriage, I took charge of my own affairs and my palliative care nurse practice, with all its difficulties. It became my life.

This chakra is associated with other physical symptoms, such as issues in the mouth, teeth, and thyroid. My small grandchildren would be intrigued with all the gold crowns in my mouth. Thyroid function has also been a concern. Some events in life can be difficult to swallow, and at times I realised that I was inadequate and restricted in expressing myself. I had many ideas about putting holistic care into place and forming a community of nurses and carers in which they could grow. The monthly in-service education focussed on understanding self, loss, and grief, and ways to communicate effectively with the knowledge of personality and cultural differences. My passion for self-awareness and excellence was not always appreciated, and to share the burden of responsibility I went through a process of accreditation and formalising the Policy and Procedure Manuals. In this way, when things didn't go the way an employee or client expected, the Policy and Procedures were a starting point in developing strategies for continuous improvement. It was a method of examining the facts without distracting emotions.

Opportunities were given to debrief situations experienced in all areas of case management. One of my nun friends used to tell me that people who are hurting may unconsciously project their hurt emotions onto others. Those in our care were hurting from a multitude of life experiences. The hurt may have been physical in nature, but more often it was the emotional or spiritual hurts that were difficult to express. In some cases, there were parents who had disinherited a child for being disobedient. I nursed in an era when the eldest child was meant to follow in the father's footsteps and daughters were meant to make good marriages, rather than be their authentic selves. Members of the caring team had their own hurts that needed expression. The soul speaks through the body and the emotions.

THE SIXTH CHAKRA IS THE THIRD EYE CHAKRA.

This area between the eyebrows is the centre which bypasses the senses and receives knowing in an irrational way. It is the centre of intuition or deep knowing. Deepak Chopra, the author who demystifies the mysteries of the universe, writes that this chakra is a spiritual chakra, which leads to inner knowledge and guidance. When it is open it can enable clairvoyance, telepathy, lucid dreaming, expanded imagination, and visualisation. I learned the value of visualiation in my nursing work.

For me, the support of a person who is dying is much more than traditional medical and nursing care. It is also care of the soul. I relate to the idea of being a midwife to the soul. An object that gave connection to the third chakra for one frail elderly lady was a small wooden holding cross, which she kept under a pillow. Others found that connection by contemplating a mountain or a sunset or sunrise. Still others found it walking on the shoreline and listening to the sounds of the sea. I find that insights come in those still moments of meditative silence, especially on waking. I often say that God didn't speak to mankind just once when the Bible and other holy books were written. Rather, guidance and wisdom are evolving, and we experience being co-creators.

For some people, guidance comes through divination tools such as the I Ching, which originated in China more than 3000 years ago. This is not a book of fortune-telling, or intended to replace common sense, but is used for guidance when there is indecision about which direction to take. C. G. Jung described the I Ching as a method of knowing what was in the unconscious by the principle of synchronicity or meaningful coincidences that were somehow orchestrated by unseen energy. Tarot readings which use an ancient deck of cards to help a person find answers to their most important questions in life are also used by some people for guidance. However, Esoteric Philosophy teaches caution in evaluating the messages from psychics, as they may be coming from the instinctual realm rather than a higher realm. The instinctual realm is understood when animals head for higher ground long before a tsunami hits the shore.

I have had many occasions to trust inner guidance or intuition. I sometimes found myself turning onto a particular road without knowing why. Then, remembering a patient, decided to make a visit and found that it was just the right moment for me to be there. Another occasion was when I didn't heed inner guidance, and went to visit a person in my mind, I was told that they had already died. Even in my early nursing days in Toronto, I remember being conscious of the need to check on a patient recovering from surgery. It turns out that there was a complication, and the visit to the hospital room was timely for the patient's survival. Nurses have many such stories. As a mother of four small children, I have been intuitively guided to seek medical care for a child with a sore ear, and to rescue a three-year-old who had climbed onto the top of the refrigerator. Intuition and guarding angels have guided my life.

Imagination is also an effective tool for reframing past events. I was touched by an exercise in forgiveness I received while attending a retreat. In the guided meditation, we were asked to walk across a field of green grass. Tiny flowers grew in the grass. We were encouraged to gather these wild flowers and form them into a bunch. Carrying the flowers, we entered the forest on the other side of the field. In the forest, we came across a cleared space like a fairy glen. There were logs to sit on and we were guided to this place in our mind's eye. We were encouraged to invite a person we felt we needed to forgive to sit opposite us on one of the logs. We were encouraged to talk to the person and to express our feelings of regret and to give the flowers to the person with a request for forgiveness.

Clairvoyance and insight are other gifts of the third eye chakra. Following a course in Reiki, I was told by the Reiki Master that I was to write a book. This was nearly two decades before my book *As Good As Goodbyes Get: A Window into Death and Dying* was published. I remember asking how I should write a book. I was told to write as I speak. I also remember being told to watch for signs in nature for they will have a message. A profound message was received the day I was lying on a rock by the sea. Two seagulls flew overhead in parallel flight paths. I was at a low point in my life, and when I was preparing for bed that night, I bumped the bedside table. Out flew a small book on Buddhism. On the cover were two parallel white lines, like the flight paths of the birds, and in between the lines were the words: "You are responsible." The birds drew my attention to what I needed to know. I got the message that I needed to change my thinking if I wanted other circumstances to change. Truly a message from the universe!

With intuitive third-eye guidance, I have tried to live by the ethical principle of seeking to do the greater good and to do no harm. I have appreciated the need to change my attitude. For example, changing:

- Condemnation to empathy
- Ignorance to understanding
- Resignation to acceptance
- Denial to honesty

- Resistance to flexibility
- Stagnation to willingness
- Suppression to openness
- Fear of death to faith in a cosmic One Consciousness

Physical symptoms for this chakra, I understand to include migraines, sinusitis, seizures, poor vision, and sciatica. I have experienced migraines since childhood. They were frequent just prior to starting my nurse practice, and today I seldom have one. Maybe I needed the wake up call to get my life together thirty years ago, and maybe today I am better at listening to the voice of guidance. My eyes have Fuchs Dystrophy, which causes fluid build-up and thickens the corneal tissue and fogs and swells the cornea, particularly in the morning. I have had surgery for cataracts and for a vitreous haemorrhage in my right eye, which required four surgeries to maintain sight. As if to demonstrate that I am a slow learner, I have also had shingles in my right eye. No wonder I am, today, working at unblocking energies that do not serve in this area of my life!

THE SEVENTH CHAKRA IS THE CROWN CHAKRA.

The crown chakra is a sacred place for reviewing and healing those aspects of the personality that are not aligned with the soul. It is a place where a personal relationship with the Divine, with all its inadequate names, is formed. It is a place for living in the present moment and to trust the life or soul-driven nature, and the greater cosmic landscape. It is also a place to express appreciation for all that is, and to feel unconditional love. It is a time to consider the valuable Buddhist lesson of detachment. How often I have told myself and others that pain and suffering comes with attachment and aversion.

In my pursuit of Buddhist wisdom, I learned about an exercise for a person who is dying. The exercise involves the person holding the image of their essence as a pearl. The pearl travels up and down on the breath in an imagined tube that joins the heart and the crown chakra. The person also imagines the crown chakra opening with each breath and, when the time is right, God by whatever name, will harvest the pearl. This exercise reminds me of another birth. Exercises focusing on the breath were also encouraged in childbirth. Birth and death are one.

I have been guided to this place of detachment and am keen to go through transition in a gracious and mentoring way. Death is just another level of understanding. My legacy is to remove the fear of death and to change the accustomed belief that disease and death are tragic. Love and fear are two switches, which cannot both be on at the same time!

How will I die? I believe that I am in the care of my unseen guides who have been with me in my intuitive thoughts, dreams, and urgings. Just as I can be the observer of my emotions and thoughts once the physical body is no more, I can also meditate on being the observer of the soul melting into spaciousness.

The seventh chakra for me is about having a sense of God as the Creator, about moral achievement, accepting self in order to accept others and about "reaching the unreachable star and fighting for right..." These are the lyrics of a famous song sung by Elvis Presley, Frank Sinatra, and more.

> And I know if I'll only be true
> To this glorious quest
> That my heart will be peaceful and calm
> When I'm laid to my rest

That song describes my star sign, which is Sagittarius. When I heard it being played on the website of Heidi Rose Robbins I felt at home! Being a palliative care nurse has afforded me many opportunities to glimpse into the world beyond this life. Mostly, I have learned that death is not only a medical concern. It is a soul concern. It is the completion of a cycle of energy. What is needed is a clear lens to look through when viewing the big issues of life and its meaning. Too often, the lens is cloudy or distorted by one's own prejudices and perceptions acquired in the base chakra.

Uncovering the hidden parts of our soul is shadow work. By shining a light on this dense darkness, or heavy energy, the energy can be dissipated and healed. I have found that by looking at a person deeply I see many of the hidden parts of my life when I see what I like and what I do not like in that person. The soul seems to choose what it needs to evolve by introducing mentors. When the student is ready, the teacher appears, is a worthy mantra.

I feel my greatest change is a change of attitude to view events with non-attachment to the outcome. Things are as they are. It is my attitude that can change when circumstances cannot. The expression 'being grounded' is heard when someone or something doesn't seem practical or real. One thing that is real is our body. It houses the soul during this earthly period. It has been said that the body is a portal into the soul. I can accept that this notion is helpful in meditation, as well as noticing what parts of the body are needing me to take notice of them. I can feel myself entering the body as a prelude to meditation.

The seventh chakra is the threshold for "parting the veil" between this world and the next. A blockage in this chakra may result in a disease affecting the brain and the whole body. A sleep disorder can also be an issue, along with depression and a sense of meaninglessness. While I normally sleep well, there are nights when I say that someone is walking over my soul and no matter what I try, I cannot fall asleep. Many years ago, I was introduced to Pranic Healing based on the work of Grand Master Choa Kok Sui. This work teaches ways to cleanse the chakras and to heal the body with an ancient science and art of healing that uses prana or life energy. I feel that energy medicine will play an important role in the future of personal health and wellness. There is much to learn in this mystery we call life.

I do know that how the threshold of death is approached will be the difference between living a life of conscious choices and feeling that the personality has grown in line with the soul's destiny, and despair.

Death is the mirror of life.

—Thomas Hubl

SOME BOOKS THAT HAVE INFLUENCED MY LIFE

Alexander, Eben. 2013 Proof of Heaven. New York: Simon and Schuster.

Armstrong, Karen. 1993 *A History of God,* Great Britain: William Heinemann Ltd.

Augsberger, David. 1981 *Caring Enough to Forgive.* California: Regal Books

Baginski, Bodo, J. 1988 *Reiki-Universal Life Energy.* USA: Life Rhythm

Bailey, Alice, A. 2015 *Death: The Great Adventure,* USA: Lucis Publishing Company.

Barbato, Michael. 2009 *Reflections on a* Setting *Sun.* Australia: Griffin Press.

Bowker, John. 1993. Canto Edition. *The meaning of death.* UK: Cambridge Uni. Press.

Beauchamp, Tom, L. Childress, James, F. 1989 *Principles of Biomedical Ethics.* USA: *Oxford* University Press.

Burdman, Geri Marr. 2008. *Search for Significance – Finding Meaning in Times of Change, Challenge and Chaos.* USA: Bellevue Press.

Buzan, Tony. 2001 *The Power of Spiritual Intelligence.* UK: Thorsons.

Chopra, Deepak. 2006 *Life After Death – The Burden of Proof.* USA: Harmony Books.

Briggs Myers, Isabel and Myers, Peter. 1995 *Gifts Differing – Understanding Personality Type.* USA: *Consulting* Psychologists Press.

Calabria, Michael D, and Janet A. Macrae. 1994. *Suggestions for thought by Florence Nightingale.* Philadelphia: University of Pennsylvania.

Chodron, Pema. 1991. *The Wisdom of no Escape and a Path to Loving Kindness.* USA: Shambala.

Chodron, Yeshe. 2004 *Everyday* Enlightenment *– how to be a spiritual warrior at the kitchen sink.* USA: Harper Collins Publishers.

Chopra, Deepak. 1993. *Ageless Body, Timeless Mind.* New York, USA: Harmony Books

Cilento, R. 1993. *Heal Cancer: Choose your own survival path.* Melbourne, Australia: Hill of Content Publishing Company, Pty Ltd.

Cohen, Misha Ruth, and Kalia Doner. 1996. *The Chinese way in healing: Many paths to wholeness.* USA: The Berkley Publishing Co.

Corey, Gerald. 1996 *Theory and Practice of Counseling and Psychotherapy, Fifth Edition.* USA: Brooks/Cole Publishing Company.

Dalai Lama, Desmond Tutu, Douglas Abrams. 2016. *The Book of Joy – Lasting Happiness in a Changing World.* UK: Penguin Random House.

Dening, Sarah. 1995. *The Everyday I Ching.* USA: St Martin's Press.

Dossey, Larry.1989. *Recovering the soul: A scientific and spiritual search.* New York, USA: Bantam Books.

Dossey, Larry. 1991. *Meaning and Medicine.* New York, USA: Bantam Books.

Dossey, Larry. 1993. *Healing words: The power of prayer and practice of medicine.* New York, USA: Harper-Collins Francisco.

Emden, C. and J. Nugent. 1992. *Issues in* Australian *Nursing 3.* UK: Churchill Livingstone.

Erikson, E.H. 1950. *Childhood and Society.* USA: Norton

Evans-Wentz, W.Y., Ed. 1960. *The Tibetan Book of the Dead.* UK: Oxford University Press.

Fox, Matthew. 1983. *Original Blessing.* Santa Fe, New Mexico: Bear & Co.

Furth, Greg. 2003. *The Secret World of Drawings – A Jungian Approach to Healing Through Art.* Canada: Inner City Books.

Geary, B. and J. Zeig. 2001. *The Handbook of Ericksonian Psychotherapy.* Phoenix, Arizona: The Milton H. Erickson Foundation Press.

Gibran, Kahlil. 1926. *The Prophet.* UK: Heinemann Ltd.

Goldner, Diane. 1999. *How People Heal: Exploring the Scientific Basis of Subtle Energy Healing.* Charlottesville, Virginia: Hampton Roads Publishing Company, Inc.

Griffiths, Bede. 1982. *The Marriage of East and West.* UK: William Collins.

Griffiths, Bede. 1990. *Return to the Centre.* India: Saccidananda Ashram, Shantivanam.

Harvey, Andrew. 2006 *A Walk with Four Spiritual Guides – Krishna, Buddha, Jesus and Ramakrishna.* USA: Skylight Paths Publishing.

Hay, Louise. 1987. *You Can Heal Your Life.* USA: Hay House.

Houston, Jean. 1982. *The Possible Person – A Course in Enhancing Your Physical, Mental and Creative Abilities.* California, USA: Jeremy Tarcher Inc.

Holecek, Andrew. 2013 *Preparing to Die – Practical Advice and Spiritual Wisdom from the Tibetan Buddhist Tradition,* Snow Lion, USA & UK

Johnson, R. 1983. *We: Understanding the Psychology of Romantic Love.* New York, USA: Harper and Row.

Johnson, R. 1989. *She: Understanding Feminine Psychology.* Revised Edition. New York, USA: Harper and Row.

Johnson, R. 1989. *He: Understanding Masculine Psychology.* Revised Edition. New York, USA: Harper and Row.

Johnson, R. 1991. *Owning Your Own Shadow.* New York, USA: HarperCollins Publishers.

Jung, Carl, G. 1969. *Man and His Symbols.* Garden City, NY, USA: Doubleday.

Kehoe, John. 1987. *Mind Power.* West Vancouver, Canada: Zoetic Inc.

Kornfield, Jack. 1994. *A Path with Heart – A Guide Through the Perils and Promises of Spiritual Life.* USA: Bantam Books.

Kornfield, Jack. 2000. *After the Ecstasy, The Laundry.* USA: Bantam Books.

Kessler, David. 2010 *Visions, Trips, and Crowded Rooms – Who and What You See Before You Die.* USA: Hay House Inc.

Krieger, Dolores. 1992 *The Therapeutic Touch – How to use your hands to help or to heal.* USA: Fireside.

Krieger, Dolores. 1993 *Accepting Your Power to Heal – The Personal Practice of Therapeutic Touch.* USA: Bear & Co.

Kubler-Ross, Elisabeth. 1969. *On Death and Dying.* London: Tavistock.

Kubler-Ross, Elisabeth. 1975 *Death: The Final Stage of Growth.* UK: Spectrum Books.

Kubler-Ross, Elisabeth. Kessler, David. 2001 *Life Lessons – How our Mortality can Teach us about Life and Death.* UK: Simon & Schuster.

Kuhl, David. 2005 *What Dying People Want – Practical Wisdom for the End of Life.* Australia: Griffin Press.

Kunz, Dora van Gelder. 1991. *The Personal Aura.* Wheaton, Illinois: Quest Books.

Lamerton, Richard. 1990 *Care of the Dying.* UK: Penguin Group.

Longaker, Christine. 2001 *Facing Death and Finding Hope.* USA: Broadway Books.

Macrae, Janet. 1988 *Therapeutic Touch – A practical guide*. USA: Alfred A Knopf Inc.

Moore, Thomas 2010 *Care of the Soul in Medicine – Healing Guidance for Patients, Families, and the People Who Care for Them*. USA: Hay House.

Maslow, Abraham. 1971. *The Farther Reaches of Human Nature*. New York, USA: Viking.

Meares, Ainslie. 1967. *Relief Without Drugs*. UK: Souvenir Press Ltd.

Moore, Thomas. 2010. *Care of the Soul in Medicine*. California: Hay House.

Moody, R. 1976. *Life After Life*. NY, USA: Bantam Books.

Myss, Caroline. 2007 *Entering the Castle – an Inner Path to God and Your Soul*. UK: Simon & Schuster.

Myss, Caroline. 2003 *Sacred Contracts*. USA: Three Rivers Press.

Newton, Michael. 2007 *Destiny of Souls – New Case Studies of Life between Lives*. USA: Llewellyn Publications.

Orloff, Judith, MD. 2000. *Guide to Intuitive Healing*. NY, USA: Three Rivers Press.

Palmer, Helen. 1988 *The Enneagram: Understanding Yourself and the Others in Your Life*. USA: HarpersCollins.

Redfield, James. 1993 *The Celestine Prophecy*. USA: Bantam Books.

Remen, Rachel, N. 1996. *Kitchen Table Wisdom: Stories That Heal*. USA: Riverhead Books.

Rinpoche, Sogyal. 1992 *The Tibetan Book of Living and Dying*. UK: Random House.

Roach, M. Simone, CSM. 1997. *Caring from the Heart: The Convergence of Caring and Spirituality*. USA: Paulist Press.

Schulz, Mona Lisa with Hay, Louise 2016 *Heal Your Mind – Your Prescription for Wholeness through Medicine, Affirmations, and Intuition*. USA: Hay House.

Siegal, Bernie, S. 1998. *Love, Medicine and Miracles*. USA: William Morrow.

Simonton, O. Carl. 1992. *Getting Well Again*. USA: Bantam Books.

Simos, Miriam and O'Brien, Aline. 1997 *The Pagan Book of Living and dying*. USA: HarperCollins.

Sutherland, C. 1992 *Transformed by the Light: Life After Near Death*. Australia: Bantam Books.

Sutherland, C. 1995 *Children of the Light*. Australia: Bantam Books.

Tacey, David. 2003. *The Spirituality Revolution: The Emergence of Contemporary Spirituality*. Australia: HarperCollins Publishers.

Tolle, Eckhart. 2004. *The Power of Now-A Guide to Spiritual Enlightenment.* Australia: Hodder.

Tolle, Eckhart. 2005. *A new Earth – Create a Bette Life.* Australia: Penguin Group.

Webb, Val. 2002. *Florence Nightingale – The Making of a Radical Theologian.* USA: Chalice Press.

Weiss, Brian. 1988. *Many Lives, Many Masters.* Fireside. USA: Simon and Schuster.

Westburg, Granger, E. 2011. *Good Grief.* USA: Fortress Press.

White, John. 1988. *A Practical Guide to Death and Dying.* USA: The theosophical Publishing House.

ABOUT THE AUTHOR

Joy Nugent received training in nursing and midwifery in Australia and Scotland and worked as a nurse in Toronto, Canada, and in London, England, over the course of her career. She pioneered a private nurse practice for three decades and founded NurseLink Foundation, a non-profit public company with charitable status providing end-of-life education and nursing services.

She is the author of: As Good As Goodbyes Get – A Window into Death and Dying and My Way – One Nurse's Passion for End of Life.

This book shares not only Nugent's personal soul journey but refers to her model for end-of-life nursing. Although she has had to face many challenges and struggles along the way, she acknowledges that her life has been divinely guided.

Nugent says, "The soul is the part of us that does not die and needs consideration along with keeping the physical body comfortable. Soul care is the essence of end-of-life care – more than that - it is the reason we were born."

She currently lives in Adelaide where she is the Patron and Founder of Soul Talks Inc. This organisation promotes self-healing and encouragement is given to raising the level of consciousness within individual participants by means of sharing personal and professional journeys.

Printed in the United States
By Bookmasters